DASH Diet Recipes for Lifelong Wellness

Embark on a Flavorful Journey to Improved Health with Wholesome, Low-Sodium Recipes

Chloe Harrison

Copyright © 2023 - All rights reserved.

The content contained within this book may not be reproduced, duplicated, or transmitted without direct written permission from the author or the publisher.

Under no circumstances will any blame or legal responsibility be held against the publisher, or author, for any damages, reparation, or monetaryloss due to the information contained within this book. Either directly or indirectly.

Legal Notice:

This book is copyright protected. This book is only for personal use. You cannot amend, distribute, sell, use, quote, or paraphrase any part, or the content within this book, without the consent of the author or publisher.

Disclaimer Notice:

Please note the information contained within this document is for educational and entertainment purposes only. All effort has been executed to present accurate, up-to-date, and reliable, complete information. No warranties of any kind are declared or implied. Readers acknowledge that the author is not engaging in the rendering of legal, financial, medical, or professional advice. The content within this book has been derived from various sources. Please consult a licensed professional before attempting any techniques outlined in this book.

By reading this document, the reader agrees that under no circumstances is the author responsible for any losses, direct or indirect, which are incurred as a result of the use of the information contained within this document, including, but not limited to, — errors, omissions, or inaccuracies.

Table of Contents

INTRODUCTION

Welcome to the exciting realm of the DASH diet! If you've stumbled upon this, you're probably eager to boost your health, consume more nutrient-rich foods, and lead an exceptional life. You've come to the right place.

The DASH diet has existed for several decades, but it's only recently that it has gained widespread recognition. And for a good reason: this dietary plan is not only delectable but also incredibly healthful.

It has demonstrated effectiveness in reducing blood pressure, decreasing the risk of heart disease and stroke, and promoting overall wellness.

So, what exactly is the DASH diet? It stands for Dietary Approaches to Stop Hypertension and was initially created by the National Heart, Lung, and Blood Institute (NHLBI) to help people lower their blood pressure without medication. This diet emphasizes whole, nutrient-dense foods and minimizes processed and high-sodium foods.

The core tenets of the DASH diet are simple: consume a variety of whole, nutrient-rich foods and products; limit processed foods, saturated fats, and added sugars; reduce sodium intake by selecting low-sodium alternatives and avoiding high-sodium foods; and balance calorie intake with physical activity to achieve and maintain a healthy weight.

The DASH diet isn't a one-size-fits-all solution, nor is it about counting calories or eliminating entire food groups. Instead, it's about making healthy choices and crafting a balanced diet that suits you.

This is where this book comes into play. It contains a diverse collection of delicious, healthy recipes following the DASH diet principles. Not only are these recipes good for you, but they're also mouthwatering. We've got you covered from breakfast to dinner, snacks to desserts.

Creating these recipes was a challenge, and my goal was to ensure each dish was both healthy and flavorful. I tested and retested each recipe until I was confident it was perfect, and I included a wide array of dishes so that there is something for everyone.

The DASH diet isn't about deprivation; it's about finding equilibrium between healthy choices and indulgences. That's why you'll find a variety of delicious, comforting dishes in this book, ranging from lasagna to stir-fry and mac and cheese to chocolate cake.

Of course, I made sure each recipe adhered to the DASH diet principles, using plenty of fruits and vegetables, lean proteins such as chicken and fish, whole grains like brown rice and quinoa, and minimal added sugars and saturated fats. Additionally, I kept sodium levels in check by using a variety of herbs and spices for flavor instead of relying on salt.

The DASH diet isn't solely about the food you eat; it's also about how you eat. This includes savoring your meals, being mindful of your hunger and fullness cues, cooking at home more frequently, and planning your meals and snacks. It also involves staying active and engaging in regular exercise, such as walking, going to the gym, or trying new activities.

If you're searching for a scientifically-backed healthy eating plan to help you achieve your health objectives, the DASH diet is an excellent starting point. Not only is it delicious and satisfying, but it also offers numerous health benefits that can help you live your best life.

One of the primary advantages of the DASH diet is its capacity to lower blood pressure. High blood pressure, or hypertension, is a prevalent health issue that can increase the risk of heart disease, stroke, and other severe health conditions. The DASH diet has proven to be an effective way to lower blood pressure in individuals with hypertension and those with normal blood pressure.

Breakfast

Greek Yogurt Parfait with Berries and Granola

Preparation time: 10 minutes

Servings: 2

Ingredients:

- 1 cup of plain non-fat Greek yogurt
- 1 cup of mixed berries (such as strawberries, blueberries, or raspberries)
- 1/2 cup of low-sugar granola
- 1 tablespoon of honey (optional)

Instructions:

1. Rinse the mixed berries under running water and chop them if necessary.
2. Add a layer of Greek yogurt in two separate serving glasses or jars.
3. Add a layer of mixed berries on top of the yogurt.
4. Sprinkle granola over the mixed berries to form another layer.
5. Repeat the layers until the glasses are filled, making sure to end with a layer of granola on top.
6. Drizzle honey over the top layer of granola (if using).
7. Chill the parfait in the refrigerator for 30 minutes to 1 hour.
8. Serve and enjoy!

Nutritional Values:

Calories: 205 Total Fat: 2 g Saturated Fat: 0 g Cholesterol: 3 mg Sodium: 76 mg Total Carbohydrate: 36 g Dietary Fiber: 4 g Total Sugars: 18 g Protein: 17 g

---

Berry and Spinach Smoothie Bowl

Preparation time: 5 minutes

Servings: 2

Ingredients:

- 2 cups of fresh spinach leaves
- 1 ripe banana, sliced
- 1 cup of mixed frozen berries (such as strawberries, blueberries, and raspberries)
- 1/2 cup of low-fat milk or unsweetened almond milk
- 1/2 cup of plain non-fat Greek yogurt
- 1 tablespoon of honey (optional)
- 1/4 cup of low-sugar granola
- 2 tablespoons of chia seeds (optional)

Instructions:

1. Add the spinach leaves, sliced banana, mixed frozen berries, milk, and Greek yogurt in a blender.
2. Blend the ingredients until smooth and creamy.
3. If desired, add honey to sweeten the smoothie taste.
4. Pour the smoothie into two serving bowls.

5. Top each bowl with a sprinkle of granola and chia seeds if using.

6. Serve and enjoy!

Nutritional Values:

Calories: 210 Total Fat: 3 g Saturated Fat: 1 g Cholesterol: 6 mg Sodium: 78 mg Total Carbohydrate: 39 g Dietary Fiber: 7 g Total Sugars: 23 g Protein: 10 g

Veggie Omelet with Spinach

Preparation time: 10 minutes

Cooking Time: 10 minutes

Servings: 2

Ingredients:

- 4 large eggs
- 1 cup of fresh spinach, chopped
- 1 medium tomato, diced
- 1/2 cup of mushrooms, sliced
- 1/4 tsp of salt
- 1/8 tsp of black pepper
- 1 tbsp of extra-virgin olive oil
- 1/4 cup of low-fat shredded cheese

Instructions:

1. In a medium bowl, beat the eggs with salt and black pepper until well combined.
2. Heat a large non-stick skillet over medium heat. Add the olive oil and swirl to coat the bottom of the skillet.
3. Add the chopped spinach, mushrooms, and diced tomatoes to the skillet. Cook, frequently stirring, for about 5 minutes or until the vegetables are tender and the excess moisture has evaporated.
4. Reduce the heat to medium-low and pour the beaten eggs over the vegetables. Tilt the skillet to ensure the eggs cover the entire surface of the skillet.
5. Sprinkle the shredded cheese over the omelet and cover it with a lid. Cook for 3-5 minutes until the eggs are set and the cheese is melted.
6. Fold the omelet in half using a spatula and slide it onto a serving plate. Serve hot.

Nutritional Values:

Calories: 227kcal Total Fat: 16g Saturated Fat: 5g Cholesterol: 347mg Sodium: 454mg Total Carbohydrate: 6g Dietary Fiber: 1g Sugar: 3g Protein: 16g

---

Sweet Potato and Black Bean Breakfast Burrito

Preparation time: 20 minutes

Cooking Time: 20 minutes

Servings: 4

Ingredients:

- 2 medium sweet potatoes peeled and diced
- 1 can of black beans, drained and rinsed
- 1 red bell pepper, diced
- 1/2 red onion, diced
- 1 tablespoon of olive oil
- 1 teaspoon of ground cumin
- 1/2 teaspoon of chili powder
- Salt and pepper, to taste
- 4 whole wheat tortillas
- 4 large eggs
- 1/2 cup of shredded low-fat cheddar cheese
- Salsa, for serving (optional)

Instructions:

1. Preheat the oven to 400°F (200°C).
2. Mix the sweet potato, black beans, red bell pepper, red onion, olive oil, ground cumin, chili powder, salt, and pepper in a large bowl.
3. Spread the mixture in a single layer on a baking sheet and roast in the oven for 20 minutes or until the sweet potatoes are tender.
4. While the sweet potato mixture is roasting, heat a non-stick skillet over medium heat.

5. Crack the eggs into the skillet and cook them to your preferred level of doneness.

6. Warm the whole wheat tortillas in the microwave or on a skillet.

7. To assemble the burritos, divide the sweet potato mixture, scrambled eggs, and shredded cheese evenly among the four tortillas.

8. Fold the tortillas up into a burrito shape.

9. Serve with salsa, if desired.

Nutritional Values:

Calories: 375 Total Fat: 13 g Saturated Fat: 4 g Cholesterol: 213 mg Sodium: 450 mg Total Carbohydrate: 47 g Dietary Fiber: 12 g Total Sugars: 7 g Protein: 21 g

---

Broccoli and Feta Frittata

Preparation time: 10 minutes

Cooking Time: 20 minutes

Servings: 4

Ingredients:

- 8 large eggs
- 1/2 cup of crumbled feta cheese
- 1 head of broccoli, chopped into small florets
- 1/2 red onion, diced
- 1 tablespoon of olive oil

- Salt and pepper, to taste

Instructions:

1. Preheat the oven to 350°F (180°C).
2. In a large bowl, whisk the eggs until frothy.
3. Add the crumbled feta cheese to the bowl and mix well.
4. In a 10-inch oven-safe skillet, heat the olive oil over medium heat.
5. Add the chopped broccoli and red onion to the skillet and sauté for 5-7 minutes until the vegetables are tender.
6. Pour the egg mixture over the sautéed vegetables.
7. Cook for 3-4 minutes, stirring gently until the edges are set.
8. Transfer the skillet to the preheated oven and bake for 10-12 minutes or until the frittata is set in the center.
9. Remove from the oven and let it cool for a few minutes.
10. Slice the frittata into wedges and serve.

Nutritional Values:

Calories: 209 Total Fat: 15 g Saturated Fat: 5 g Cholesterol: 370 mg Sodium: 361 mg Total Carbohydrate: 6 g Dietary Fiber: 2 g Total Sugars: 2 g Protein: 15 g

Avocado Toast with Poached Egg

Preparation time: 10 minutes

Cooking Time: 10 minutes

Servings: 2

Ingredients:

- 2 slices of whole-grain bread
- 1 ripe avocado
- 4 cherry tomatoes, halved
- 2 large eggs
- 1/4 tsp of salt
- 1/8 tsp of black pepper
- 1 tsp of white vinegar
- 1 tbsp of chopped fresh parsley

Instructions:

1. Toast the slices of bread until golden brown.
2. Cut the avocado in half and remove the pit. Scoop out the flesh into a bowl and mash it with a fork until smooth. Season with salt and black pepper to taste.
3. Top each slice of toast with the mashed avocado and halved cherry tomatoes.
4. Bring 2 inches of water to a simmer over medium heat in a medium pot. Add the white vinegar and stir.
5. Crack one egg into a small cup or ramekin. Using a spoon, create a whirlpool in the simmering water and gently slide the egg into the center of the vortex. Poach the egg for 2-3 minutes or until the white is set and the yolk is still runny.
6. Use a slotted spoon to carefully remove the poached egg from the water and place it on top of one of the avocado toasts. Repeat the same process with the second egg.
7. Sprinkle the chopped parsley over the avocado toast with poached eggs and serve immediately.

Nutritional Values:

Calories: 236kcal Total Fat: 14g Saturated Fat: 3g Cholesterol: 185mg Sodium: 316mg Total Carbohydrate: 19g Dietary Fiber: 7g Sugar: 2g Protein: 11g

Low-Fat Breakfast Quesadilla

Preparation time: 10 minutes

Cooking Time: 10 minutes

Servings: 2

Ingredients:

- 2 whole wheat tortillas
- 4 large eggs
- 1/2 cup of canned black beans, drained and rinsed
- 1/2 red bell pepper, diced
- 1/2 red onion, diced
- 1/2 cup of shredded low-fat cheddar cheese
- 1 tablespoon of olive oil
- Salt and pepper, to taste

Instructions:

1. In a non-stick skillet, heat the olive oil over medium heat.
2. Add the diced red bell pepper and red onion to the skillet and sauté for 5 minutes until tender.

3. Add the black beans to the skillet and cook for 1-2 minutes until heated.
4. Crack the eggs into a bowl and whisk them together.
5. Pour the eggs into the skillet with the vegetables and cook, occasionally stirring, until the eggs are scrambled and cooked through.
6. Divide the egg mixture into two portions and place each piece onto a tortilla.
7. Top each tortilla with 1/4 cup of shredded low-fat cheddar cheese.
8. Fold the tortillas in half to form a quesadilla.
9. Heat the quesadillas in a skillet over medium heat until the cheese is melted, and the tortillas are crispy.
10. Slice the quesadillas into wedges and serve.

Nutritional Values:

Calories: 395 Total Fat: 19 g Saturated Fat: 6 g Cholesterol: 380 mg Sodium: 605 mg Total Carbohydrate: 33 g Dietary Fiber: 11 g Total Sugars: 2 g Protein: 27 g

———— ◆ ————

Steel-Cut Oatmeal with Apples

Preparation time: 5 minutes

Cooking Time: 25 minutes

Servings: 4

Ingredients:

- 1 cup of steel-cut oats
- 4 cups of water
- 2 medium apples peeled and diced
- 1 teaspoon of ground cinnamon
- 1/4 cup of chopped walnuts
- 2 tablespoons of honey (optional)
- 1/2 cup of low-fat milk or unsweetened almond milk (optional)

Instructions:

1. In a medium-sized saucepan, bring the water to a boil.
2. Add the steel-cut oats to the boiling water and reduce the heat to low.
3. Simmer the oats, occasionally stirring, for 20-25 minutes or until the oats are tender and the mixture has thickened.
4. While the oats are cooking, mix the diced apples and ground cinnamon in a small bowl.
5. When the oats are cooked, stir in the apple mixture, and cook for 3-5 minutes until the apples are softened.
6. Remove the oats from the heat and stir in the chopped walnuts.
7. If desired, add honey to sweeten the oatmeal to taste.
8. Serve the oatmeal in individual bowls, and if desired, top it with a splash of low-fat milk or unsweetened almond milk.

Nutritional Values:

Calories: 225 Total Fat: 7 g Saturated Fat: 1 g Cholesterol: 0 mg Sodium: 7 mg

Total Carbohydrate: 37 g Dietary Fiber: 6 g Total Sugars: 14 g Protein: 7 g

Smoked Salmon and Cucumber

Preparation time: 10 minutes

Servings: 2

Ingredients:

- 2 slices of whole-grain bread
- 2 ounces of smoked salmon
- 1/2 English cucumber, sliced
- 2 tablespoons of low-fat cream cheese
- 1 tablespoon of chopped fresh dill
- Salt and pepper, to taste
- Lemon wedges for serving (optional)

Instructions:

1. Toast the slices of whole-grain bread until crispy.
2. Mix the low-fat cream cheese and chopped fresh dill in a small bowl until well combined.
3. Spread the cream cheese mixture onto the toasted bread slices.
4. Top each bread slice with slices of smoked salmon and sliced cucumber.
5. Season with salt and pepper to taste.
6. Serve with lemon wedges on the side, if desired.

Nutritional Values:

Calories: 183 Total Fat: 6 g Saturated Fat: 2 g Cholesterol: 20 mg Sodium: 418 mg Total Carbohydrate: 19 g Dietary Fiber: 4 g Total Sugars: 3 g Protein: 16 g

Whole-Grain Banana Pancakes

Preparation time: 15 minutes

Cooking Time: 15 minutes

Servings: 4

Ingredients:

- 1 cup of whole-grain flour
- 1 tbsp of baking powder
- 1/4 tsp of salt
- 1 ripe banana, mashed
- 1 cup of low-fat milk
- 1 large egg
- 1 tbsp of canola oil
- 2 tbsp of natural peanut butter
- 2 tbsp of honey

Instructions:

1. Whisk together the whole-grain flour, baking powder, and salt in a large bowl.
2. Whisk together the mashed banana, low-fat milk, egg, and canola oil in a separate bowl until smooth.

3. Add the wet ingredients to the dry ingredients and stir until well combined.

4. Heat a large non-stick skillet or griddle over medium-high heat. Use a ladle or measuring cup to pour the pancake batter onto the skillet, making 4–5-inch pancakes.

5. Cook the pancakes for 2-3 minutes or until bubbles form on the surface and the edges start to look dry. Flip the pancakes and cook for 1-2 minutes or until golden brown.

6. Serve the whole-grain banana pancakes with a dollop of natural peanut butter and a drizzle of honey on top.

Nutritional Values:

Calories: 276kcal Total Fat: 9g Saturated Fat: 1g Cholesterol: 41mg Sodium: 456mg Total Carbohydrate: 44g Dietary Fiber: 4g Sugar: 19g Protein: 8g

Cottage Cheese and Berry Breakfast Bowl

Preparation time: 5 minutes

Servings: 2

Ingredients:

- 1 cup of low-fat cottage cheese
- 1 cup of mixed berries (such as strawberries, blueberries, or raspberries)
- 1/4 cup of chopped walnuts

- 2 tablespoons of honey (optional)

Instructions:

1. Rinse the mixed berries under running water and chop them if necessary.
2. In two separate serving bowls, add a layer of low-fat cottage cheese.
3. Add a layer of mixed berries on top of the cottage cheese.
4. Sprinkle chopped walnuts over the mixed berries to form another layer.
5. If desired, drizzle honey over the top of the bowl.
6. Serve and enjoy!

Nutritional Values:

Calories: 205 Total Fat: 7 g Saturated Fat: 1 g Cholesterol: 7 mg Sodium: 423 mg Total Carbohydrate: 23 g Dietary Fiber: 4 g Total Sugars: 18 g Protein: 16 g

Chia Seed Pudding with Almond Milk

Preparation time: 5 minutes

Cooking Time: 0 minutes (refrigeration time required)

Servings: 2

Ingredients:

- 1/4 cup of chia seeds
- 1 cup of unsweetened almond milk

- 1 tbsp of honey
- 1/2 tsp of vanilla extract
- 1 cup of fresh mixed berries (such as strawberries, blueberries, and raspberries)

Instructions:

1. In a medium bowl, whisk together the chia seeds, unsweetened almond milk, honey, and vanilla extract until well combined.
2. Let the mixture rest for 5 minutes, then whisk again to prevent clumping.
3. Cover the bowl with plastic wrap and refrigerate for at least 2 hours or overnight.
4. Before serving, divide the chia seed pudding into two bowls or glasses.
5. Top each bowl or glass with a cup of fresh mixed berries.
6. Serve the chia seed pudding with almond milk and fresh fruit immediately.

Nutritional Values:

Calories: 182kcal Total Fat: 7g Saturated Fat: 1g Cholesterol: 0mg Sodium: 91mg Total Carbohydrate: 25g Dietary Fiber: 12g Sugar: 10g Protein: 6g

LUNCH

Mediterranean Quinoa Salad

Preparation time: 15 minutes

Cooking Time: 20 minutes

Servings: 4

Ingredients:

- 1 cup of uncooked quinoa
- 2 cups of water
- 1/2 cup of chopped fresh parsley
- 1/2 cup of chopped fresh mint
- 1/2 cup of crumbled feta cheese
- 1/2 cup of chopped Kalamata olives
- 1/4 cup of chopped red onion
- 2 tablespoons of extra-virgin olive oil
- 2 tablespoons of red wine vinegar
- Salt and pepper, to taste

Instructions:

1. Rinse the quinoa under cold water.
2. In a medium saucepan, bring the water and quinoa to a boil.
3. Reduce the heat to low and cover the saucepan.
4. Simmer for 15-20 minutes or until the quinoa is tender and the water has been absorbed.
5. In a large mixing bowl, stir the cooked quinoa, chopped fresh parsley, chopped fresh mint, crumbled feta cheese, chopped Kalamata olives, and chopped red onion.

6. Whisk together the extra-virgin olive oil and red wine vinegar in a small mixing bowl.
7. Pour the dressing over the quinoa mixture and toss until well combined.
8. Season with salt and pepper to taste.
9. Serve chilled or at room temperature and enjoy!

Nutritional Values:

Calories: 301 Total Fat: 16 g Saturated Fat: 5 g Cholesterol: 22 mg Sodium: 482 mg Total Carbohydrate: 29 g Dietary Fiber: 4 g Total Sugars: 2 g Protein: 10 g

Turkey and Avocado Lettuce Wraps

Preparation time: 15 minutes

Cooking Time: 0 minutes

Servings: 4

Ingredients:

- 1 pound of deli-sliced turkey breast
- 2 ripe avocados pitted and sliced
- 4 large lettuce leaves washed and dried
- 1/4 cup of low-fat plain Greek yogurt
- 1/4 cup of chopped fresh cilantro
- 1 tablespoon of lime juice
- Salt and pepper, to taste

Instructions:

1. Lay out the lettuce leaves on a cutting board or work surface.
2. In a mixing bowl, stir the low-fat plain Greek yogurt, chopped fresh cilantro, lime juice, salt, and pepper.
3. Spread the yogurt mixture evenly over each lettuce leaf.
4. Place a few slices of deli-sliced turkey breast and sliced avocado on top of the yogurt mixture.
5. Roll up each lettuce leaf tightly to form a wrap.
6. Serve and enjoy!

Nutritional Values:

Calories: 232 Total Fat: 13 g Saturated Fat: 2 g Cholesterol: 42 mg Sodium: 574 mg Total Carbohydrate: 9 g Dietary Fiber: 5 g Total Sugars: 2 g Protein: 21 g

Lentil Soup with Whole-Grain Bread

Preparation time: 10 minutes

Cooking Time: 40 minutes

Servings: 6

Ingredients:

- 1 tablespoon of olive oil
- 1 medium onion, chopped
- 2 cloves of garlic, minced

- 2 celery stalks, chopped
- 2 carrots, chopped
- 1/2 teaspoon of ground cumin
- 1/2 teaspoon of ground coriander
- 1/2 teaspoon of ground turmeric
- 1/2 teaspoon of paprika
- 1/4 teaspoon of ground cinnamon
- 1/4 teaspoon of cayenne pepper (optional)
- 1 cup of dry brown lentils rinsed and drained
- 6 cups of low-sodium vegetable broth
- 1 bay leaf
- Salt and pepper, to taste
- 4 slices of whole-grain bread, toasted and cut into cubes
- Chopped fresh parsley or cilantro for garnish

Instructions:

1. In a large pot, heat the olive oil over medium heat.
2. Add the chopped onion, minced garlic, celery, and carrots to the pot.
3. Cook for 5-7 minutes or until the vegetables are tender.
4. Add the ground cumin, coriander, turmeric, paprika, ground cinnamon, and cayenne pepper (if used) to the pot.
5. Cook for 1-2 minutes or until fragrant.
6. Add the rinsed and drained brown lentils, low-sodium vegetable broth, and bay leaf to the pot.
7. Bring the soup to a boil, then reduce the heat to low and simmer for 30-35 minutes or until the lentils are tender.
8. Remove the bay leaf from the soup and discard.

- Season with salt and pepper to taste.
- Ladle the soup into bowls and top with the toasted whole-grain bread cubes.
- Garnish with chopped fresh parsley or cilantro, if desired.
- Serve and enjoy!

Nutritional Values:

Calories: 228 Total Fat: 4 g Saturated Fat: 0.5 g Cholesterol: 0 mg Sodium: 198 mg Total Carbohydrate: 36 g Dietary Fiber: 14 g Total Sugars: 4 g Protein: 13 g

———— ◆ ————

Grilled Chicken and Veggie Skewers

Preparation time: 20 minutes

Cooking Time: 20 minutes

Servings: 4

Ingredients:

- 1-pound boneless, skinless chicken breasts cut into chunks
- 1 zucchini, sliced into rounds
- 1 red bell pepper, cut into chunks
- 1 yellow bell pepper, cut into chunks
- 1 red onion, cut into chunks
- 2 tablespoons olive oil
- 2 tablespoons balsamic vinegar
- 1 tablespoon honey

- 1 teaspoon Dijon mustard
- Salt and pepper, to taste
- 1 cup brown rice, cooked according to package directions

Instructions:

1. Preheat the grill to medium-high heat.
2. Whisk together the olive oil, balsamic vinegar, honey, Dijon mustard, salt, and pepper in a small bowl to make the marinade.
3. Thread the chicken and vegetables onto skewers.
4. Brush the skewers with the marinade, making sure to coat all sides.
5. Grill the skewers for 10-12 minutes, flipping once until the chicken is cooked and the vegetables are tender.
6. Serve the skewers over brown rice.

Nutritional Values:

Calories: 374 kcal Total Fat: 10g Saturated Fat: 2g Cholesterol: 65mg Sodium: 144mg Total Carbohydrate: 41g Dietary Fiber: 5g Sugar: 9g Protein: 31g

Roasted Vegetable and Hummus Wrap

Preparation time: 15 minutes

Cooking Time: 25 minutes

Servings: 4

Ingredients:

- 1 medium zucchini, sliced
- 1 red bell pepper, sliced
- 1 yellow bell pepper, sliced
- 1 red onion, sliced
- 2 tablespoons of olive oil
- Salt and pepper, to taste
- 4 large whole-grain tortillas
- 1/2 cup of hummus
- 2 cups of baby spinach leave
- 1/4 cup of crumbled feta cheese

Instructions:

1. Preheat the oven to 425°F (220°C).
2. In a large mixing bowl, toss together the sliced zucchini, red bell pepper, yellow bell pepper, red onion, olive oil, salt, and pepper.
3. Spread the vegetables out in a single layer on a large baking sheet.
4. Roast in the oven for 20-25 minutes or until the vegetables are tender and lightly browned.
5. Lay out the whole-grain tortillas on a work surface.
6. Spread 2 tablespoons of hummus evenly over each tortilla.
7. Top each tortilla with a handful of baby spinach leaves and an equal number of roasted vegetables.
8. Sprinkle the crumbled feta cheese over the vegetables.
9. Roll up each tortilla tightly to form a wrap.

10. Serve and enjoy!

Nutritional Values:

Calories: 362 Total Fat: 18 g Saturated Fat: 3 g Cholesterol: 8 mg
Sodium: 627 mg Total Carbohydrate: 41 g Dietary Fiber: 10 g Total
Sugars: 7 g Protein: 12 g

Tuna and White Bean Salad with Lemon Dressing

Preparation time: 10 minutes

Cooking Time: none

Servings: 3

Ingredients:

- 2 cans (5 oz each) of tuna in water, drained
- 2 cans (15 oz each) of white beans, rinsed and drained
- 1 red bell pepper, chopped
- 1 small red onion thinly sliced
- 1/4 cup fresh parsley, chopped
- 1/4 cup fresh lemon juice
- 2 tablespoons extra-virgin olive oil
- 1 clove garlic, minced
- Salt and pepper to taste

Instructions:

1. Combine the drained tuna, white beans, chopped red bell pepper, thinly sliced red onion, and chopped parsley in a large bowl.
2. In a small bowl, whisk together the fresh lemon juice, extra-virgin olive oil, minced garlic, salt, and pepper until well combined.
3. Pour the lemon dressing over the tuna and white bean mixture and toss until well coated.
4. Serve the salad chilled or at room temperature.

Nutritional Values:

Calories: 364 kcal Protein: 28 g Fat: 12 g Carbohydrates: 38 g Fiber: 11 g Sodium: 386 mg

---

Chickpea and Roasted Vegetable Salad

Preparation time: 15 minutes

Cooking Time: 25 minutes

Servings: 4 For the Salad:

Ingredients:

- 1 can of chickpeas rinsed and drained
- 1 red bell pepper, sliced
- 1 yellow bell pepper, sliced
- 1 small red onion, sliced
- 2 cups of baby spinach leave

- 1/4 cup of chopped fresh parsley
- Salt and pepper, to taste
- 1 tablespoon of olive oil

For the Dressing:

- 2 tablespoons of balsamic vinegar
- 1 tablespoon of honey
- 1 tablespoon of Dijon mustard
- 1 tablespoon of olive oil
- Salt and pepper, to taste

Instructions:

1. Preheat the oven to 425°F (220°C).
2. In a large mixing bowl, toss the rinsed and drained chickpeas, sliced red bell pepper, sliced yellow bell pepper, sliced red onion, olive oil, salt, and pepper.
3. Spread the vegetables out in a single layer on a large baking sheet.
4. Roast in the oven for 20-25 minutes or until the vegetables are tender and lightly browned.
5. Whisk together the balsamic vinegar, honey, Dijon mustard, olive oil, salt, and pepper in a small mixing bowl to make the dressing.
6. Toss the roasted vegetables, baby spinach leaves, and chopped fresh parsley in a large mixing bowl.
7. Drizzle the balsamic dressing over the salad and toss to combine.
8. Divide the salad evenly among 4 plates.

9. Serve and enjoy!

Nutritional Values:

Calories: 192 Total Fat: 7 g Saturated Fat: 1 g Cholesterol: 0 mg Sodium: 192 mg Total Carbohydrate: 29 g Dietary Fiber: 7 g Total Sugars: 12 g Protein: 7 g

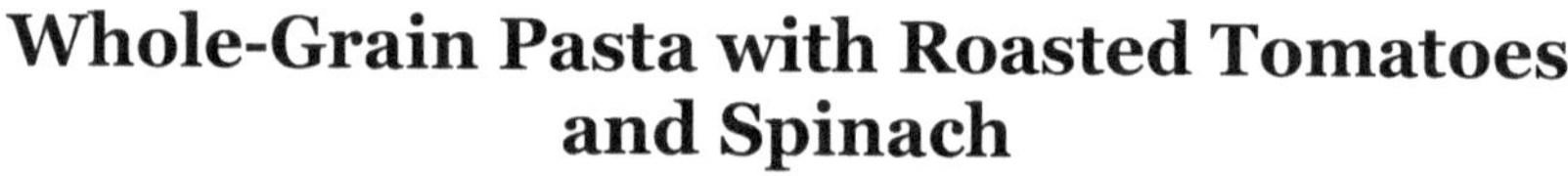

Whole-Grain Pasta with Roasted Tomatoes and Spinach

Preparation time: 10 minutes

Cooking Time: 20 minutes

Servings: 4

Ingredients:

- 12 ounces of whole-grain pasta
- 2 pints of cherry tomatoes, halved
- 4 cloves of garlic, minced
- 2 tablespoons of olive oil
- Salt and pepper, to taste
- 4 cups of baby spinach leave
- 1/4 cup of grated Parmesan cheese

Instructions:

1. Preheat the oven to 400°F (200°C).

2. In a large mixing bowl, toss together the halved cherry tomatoes, minced garlic, olive oil, salt, and pepper.

3. Spread the tomato mixture in a single layer on a large baking sheet.

4. Roast in the oven for 15-20 minutes or until the tomatoes are tender and lightly browned.

5. While the tomatoes are roasting, cook the whole-grain pasta according to the package instructions.

6. Drain the cooked pasta and return it to the pot.

7. Add the roasted tomato mixture and the baby spinach leaves to the pot with the pasta.

8. Toss everything together until the spinach is wilted and the pasta is coated with the tomato juices.

9. Sprinkle the grated Parmesan cheese over the pasta.

10. Serve and enjoy!

Nutritional Values:

Calories: 384 Total Fat: 10 g Saturated Fat: 2 g Cholesterol: 5 mg Sodium: 177 mg Total Carbohydrate: 62 g Dietary Fiber: 9 g Total Sugars: 7 g Protein: 14 g

Grilled Salmon with Roasted Vegetables

Preparation time: 10 minutes

Cooking Time: 20 minutes

Servings: 4

Ingredients:

- 4 salmon fillets (4-6 oz each), skin removed
- 1 large zucchini, sliced
- 1 red bell pepper, sliced
- 1 yellow bell pepper, sliced
- 1 small red onion, sliced
- 2 tablespoons olive oil
- 2 teaspoons dried basil
- Salt and pepper to taste

Instructions:

1. Preheat the oven to 400°F (200°C).
2. Arrange the sliced zucchini, red and yellow bell peppers, and red onion on a baking sheet lined with parchment paper.
3. Drizzle the vegetables with olive oil and sprinkle with dried basil, salt, and pepper.
4. Toss the vegetables until evenly coated, then spread them out in a single layer on the baking sheet.
5. Roast the vegetables in the oven for 20 minutes or until tender and slightly charred.
6. While the vegetables are roasting, heat a grill pan over medium-high heat.
7. Season the salmon fillets with salt and pepper to taste.
8. Grill the salmon for 4-5 minutes per side or until cooked through.

9. Serve the grilled salmon with the roasted vegetables on the side.

Nutritional Values:

Calories: 380 kcal Protein: 34 g Fat: 23 g Carbohydrates: 11 g Fiber: 3 g Sodium: 108 mg

---

Veggie Burger with Sweet Potato Fries

Preparation time: 30 minutes

Cooking Time: 30 minutes

Servings: 4

Ingredients:

<u>For the Veggie Burger:</u>

- 1 can of black beans rinsed and drained
- 1/2 cup of cooked brown rice
- 1/4 cup of chopped fresh cilantro
- 1/4 cup of chopped red onion
- 2 cloves of garlic, minced
- 1 teaspoon of ground cumin
- 1/2 teaspoon of smoked paprika
- Salt and pepper, to taste
- 1 egg
- 1/2 cup of whole-wheat breadcrumbs

- 4 whole-wheat buns
- 4 lettuce leaves
- 4 slices of tomato

<u>For the Sweet Potato Fries:</u>

- 2 medium sweet potatoes, peeled and cut into thin strips
- 1 tablespoon of olive oil
- 1/2 teaspoon of smoked paprika
- Salt and pepper, to taste

Instructions:

1. Preheat the oven to 400°F (200°C).
2. In a large mixing bowl, mash the rinsed and drained black beans with a fork.
3. Add the cooked brown rice, chopped cilantro, chopped red onion, minced garlic, ground cumin, smoked paprika, salt, and pepper to the bowl with the mashed black beans.
4. Stir everything together until well combined.
5. Add the egg and whole-wheat breadcrumbs to the bowl and mix until evenly distributed.
6. Form the mixture into 4 patties.
7. Place the patties on a lightly oiled baking sheet and bake in the oven for 20-25 minutes or until they are cooked and lightly browned.
8. While the veggie burgers are baking, prepare the sweet potato fries.
9. Toss the sweet potato strips, olive oil, smoked paprika, salt, and pepper in a large mixing bowl.

10. Spread the sweet potato strips in a single layer on a large baking sheet.

11. Roast in the preheated oven for 20-25 minutes, or until they are tender and lightly browned.

12. Serve the veggie burgers on whole-wheat buns with lettuce leaves, tomato slices, and sweet potato fries on the side. 13. Enjoy!

Nutritional Values:

Calories: 435 Total Fat: 10 g Saturated Fat: 2 g Cholesterol: 47 mg Sodium: 483 mg Total Carbohydrate: 72 g Dietary Fiber: 17 g Total Sugars: 13 g Protein: 18 g

---

Shrimp and Vegetable Stir-Fry with Brown Rice

Preparation time: 15 minutes

Cooking Time: 20 minutes

Servings: 4

Ingredients:

- 1-pound raw shrimp, peeled and deveined
- 3 cups cooked brown rice
- 1 red bell pepper thinly sliced
- 1 yellow bell pepper thinly sliced
- 1 small onion thinly sliced

- 2 cloves garlic, minced
- 2 tablespoons olive oil
- 1 tablespoon low-sodium soy sauce
- 1 teaspoon honey
- 1 teaspoon grated ginger
- Salt and pepper to taste

Instructions:

1. Heat a large skillet over medium-high heat. Add 1 tablespoon of olive oil to the skillet.
2. Once the oil is hot, add the shrimp to the skillet and season with salt and pepper. Cook the shrimp for 2-3 minutes on each side or until fully cooked. Remove the shrimp from the skillet and set aside.
3. Add the remaining tablespoon of olive oil to the skillet. Once hot, add the sliced onions, bell peppers, and garlic to the skillet. Cook for 5-7 minutes, stirring occasionally, or until the vegetables are tender.
4. Whisk together the soy sauce, honey, and grated ginger in a small bowl.
5. Add the cooked shrimp back into the skillet with the vegetables. Pour the soy sauce mixture over the shrimp and vegetables and toss everything together until the shrimp and vegetables are coated in the sauce.
6. Serve the shrimp and vegetable stir-fry over cooked brown rice.

Nutritional Values:

Calories: 370 kcal Fat: 9g Carbohydrates: 45g Fiber: 6g Protein: 29g Sodium: 260mg

Chicken and Vegetable Stir-Fry

Preparation time: 20 minutes

Cooking Time: 20 minutes

Servings: 4

Ingredients:

- 1 cup of brown rice
- 2 cups of water
- 1 tablespoon of olive oil
- 1 pound of boneless, skinless chicken breasts cut into bite-sized pieces
- 2 cups of sliced mixed vegetables (such as bell peppers, carrots, broccoli, and snap peas)
- 2 cloves of garlic, minced
- 1 tablespoon of grated fresh ginger
- 2 tablespoons of low-sodium soy sauce
- 1 tablespoon of rice vinegar
- 1 teaspoon of honey
- 1/4 teaspoon of red pepper flakes
- Salt and pepper, to taste

Instructions:

1. In a medium saucepan, bring the water to a boil.
2. Add the brown rice and stir well.
3. Cover the saucepan and reduce the heat to low.
4. Simmer for 45-50 minutes or until the rice is tender and all the water is absorbed.
5. While the rice is cooking, heat the olive oil in a large skillet over medium-high heat.
6. Add the chicken pieces to the skillet and cook for 5-7 minutes or until cooked.
7. Next, add the sliced vegetables, minced garlic, and grated ginger to the skillet.
8. Cook for another 5-7 minutes or until the vegetables are tender-crisp.
9. Whisk together the low-sodium soy sauce, rice vinegar, honey, red pepper flakes, salt, and pepper in a small mixing bowl.
10. Pour the sauce over the chicken and vegetables in the skillet and toss everything together until everything is evenly coated.
11. Serve the chicken and vegetable stir-fry over the cooked brown rice.
12. Enjoy!

Nutritional Values:

Calories: 330 Total Fat: 7 g Saturated Fat: 1 g Cholesterol: 65 mg Sodium:

415 mg Total Carbohydrate: 38 g Dietary Fiber: 4 g Total Sugars: 4 g Protein: 29 g

Greek Salad with Chicken and Whole-Grain Pita

Preparation time: 20 minutes

Cooking Time: 20 minutes

Servings: 4

Ingredients:

For the Greek Salad:

- 4 cups of chopped romaine lettuce
- 1 cup of sliced cucumber
- 1 cup of halved cherry tomatoes
- 1/2 cup of sliced red onion
- 1/2 cup of crumbled feta cheese
- 1/4 cup of sliced Kalamata olives

For the Chicken:

- 1 pound of boneless, skinless chicken breasts
- 2 cloves of garlic, minced
- 1 tablespoon of dried oregano
- 1 tablespoon of olive oil
- Salt and pepper, to taste

For the Whole-Grain Pita:

- whole-grain pitas

- 2 tablespoon of olive oil
- 1/4 teaspoon of garlic powder
- Salt and pepper, to taste

For the Dressing:

- 2 tablespoons of olive oil
- 1 tablespoon of red wine vinegar
- 1/2 teaspoon of dried oregano
- Salt and pepper, to taste

Instructions:

1. Preheat the oven to 400°F (200°C).
2. Combine the chopped romaine lettuce, sliced cucumber, halved cherry tomatoes, red onion, crumbled feta cheese, and sliced Kalamata olives in a large mixing bowl.
3. Toss everything together until well combined.
4. Season the chicken breasts with minced garlic, dried oregano, olive oil, salt, and pepper.
5. Place the chicken on a lightly oiled baking sheet and bake in the preheated oven for 20-25 minutes, until they are cooked through and no longer pink in the center.
6. While the chicken is baking, prepare the whole-grain pita.
7. Whisk together the olive oil, garlic powder, salt, and pepper in a small mixing bowl.
8. Brush the mixture over the surface of the whole-grain pitas.
9. Place the pitas on a baking sheet and bake in the oven for 5-7 minutes or until they are lightly browned and crispy.

10. Whisk together the olive oil, red wine vinegar, dried oregano, salt, and pepper in a small mixing bowl to make the dressing.
11. Once the chicken is done baking, slice it into bite-sized pieces.
12. Divide the Greek salad among four serving plates.
13. Top each salad with the sliced chicken.
14. Drizzle the dressing over the top of the salads.
15. Serve with the whole-grain pitas on the side.
16. Enjoy!

Nutritional Values:

Calories: 435 Total Fat: 22 g Saturated Fat: 6 g Cholesterol: 86 mg Sodium:

707 mg Total Carbohydrate: 27 g Dietary Fiber: 5 g Total Sugars: 5 g Protein: 33 g

Black Bean and Vegetable Burrito

Preparation time: 20 minutes

Cooking Time: 15 minutes

Servings: 4

Ingredients:

- 1 tablespoon olive oil
- 1 small onion, chopped

- 2 cloves garlic, minced
- 1 red bell pepper, chopped
- 1 zucchini, chopped
- 1 teaspoon ground cumin
- 1 can (15 ounces) of black beans, rinsed and drained
- 1/2 cup low-sodium vegetable broth
- 1 tablespoon lime juice
- Salt and black pepper to taste
- 4 whole wheat tortillas (8-inch)
- 1 cup shredded lettuce
- 1/2 cup salsa
- 1/4 cup chopped fresh cilantro

Instructions:

1. In a large skillet, heat the olive oil over medium heat. Add the onion and garlic and cook for 2-3 minutes until softened.
2. Add the red bell pepper, zucchini, and cumin and cook for another 5-7 minutes until the vegetables are tender.
3. Add the skillet's black beans, vegetable broth, and lime juice. Cook for 2-3 minutes until the liquid is mostly absorbed. Season with salt and black pepper to taste.
4. Warm the tortillas in a microwave or on a skillet over medium heat.
5. To assemble the burritos, place a tortilla on a plate and spoon some black bean mixture onto the center. Top with shredded lettuce, salsa, and cilantro.

6. Fold the bottom edge of the tortilla over the filling, then fold in the sides and roll up tightly.
7. Serve the burritos warm.

Nutritional Values:

Calories: 289 kcal Fat: 7.6 g Carbohydrates: 45.4 g Fiber: 11.4 g Protein: 11.4 g Sodium: 345 mg

Grilled Chicken Caesar Salad

Preparation time: 15 minutes

Cooking Time: 15 minutes

Servings: 4

Ingredients:

For the Salad:

- 1-pound boneless, skinless chicken breasts
- 8 cups chopped romaine lettuce.
- 1/2 cup freshly grated Parmesan cheese
- 1/2 cup whole-grain croutons
- Salt and pepper, to taste

For the Dressing:

- 1/4 cup plain Greek yogurt
- 1/4 cup freshly grated Parmesan cheese

- 2 tablespoons freshly squeezed lemon juice
- 2 tablespoons extra-virgin olive oil
- 2 cloves garlic, minced
- Salt and pepper, to taste

Instructions:

1. Preheat a grill or grill pan to medium-high heat.
2. Season the chicken breasts with salt and pepper.
3. Grill the chicken for 5-7 minutes per side or until cooked through and no longer pink in the center.
4. Remove the chicken from the grill and rest for 5 minutes.
5. Meanwhile, prepare the dressing.
6. In a small mixing bowl, whisk together the Greek yogurt, Parmesan cheese, lemon juice, olive oil, minced garlic, salt, and pepper until well combined.
7. Once the chicken has rested, slice it into bite-sized pieces.
8. Combine the chopped romaine lettuce, grated Parmesan cheese, and whole-grain croutons in a large mixing bowl.
9. Toss everything together until well combined.
10. Divide the salad among four serving plates.
11. Top each salad with the sliced chicken.
12. Drizzle the dressing over the top of the salads.
13. Serve immediately and enjoy!

Nutritional Values:

Calories: 295 Total Fat: 14 g Saturated Fat: 4 g Cholesterol: 74 mg Sodium: 362 mg Total Carbohydrate: 10 g Dietary Fiber: 3 g Total Sugars: 2 g Protein: 32 g

Dinner

Grilled Chicken and Vegetable Kebabs

Preparation time: 20 minutes

Cooking Time: 15 minutes

Servings: 4

Ingredients:

- 1 lb. boneless, skinless chicken breasts, cut into cubes
- 1 red bell pepper, cut into chunks
- 1 green bell pepper, cut into chunks
- 1 zucchini, cut into chunks
- 1 onion, cut into chunks
- 1/4 cup olive oil
- 2 cloves garlic, minced
- 1 tsp dried oregano
- Salt and pepper, to taste
- 2 cups cooked brown rice
- 4 cups steamed broccoli

Instructions:

1. Preheat grill to medium-high heat.
2. In a large bowl, combine chicken, bell peppers, zucchini, onion, olive oil, garlic, oregano, salt, and pepper. Toss to coat.
3. Thread chicken and vegetables onto skewers.
4. Grill skewers for 10-15 minutes, or until chicken is cooked through and vegetables are tender.

5. Serve grilled chicken and vegetable kebabs with cooked brown rice and steamed broccoli on the side.

Nutritional Values:

Calories: 400 Fat: 16g Carbohydrates: 33g Protein: 35g Sodium: 120mg Fiber: 8g

Vegetable and Lentil Curry

Preparation time: 15 minutes

Cooking Time: 30 minutes

Ingredients:

- 1 cup brown rice
- 2 cups water
- 1 tablespoon olive oil
- 1 onion, chopped
- 3 garlic cloves, minced
- 1 tablespoon grated ginger
- 2 teaspoons curry powder
- 1 teaspoon ground turmeric
- 1 teaspoon ground cumin
- 1 teaspoon ground coriander
- 1/2 teaspoon ground cinnamon
- 1/2 teaspoon ground cardamom
- 1/2 teaspoon salt
- 1 red bell pepper, chopped

- 1 zucchini, chopped
- 1 can (15 ounces) diced tomatoes
- 1 can (15 ounces) lentils rinsed and drained
- 2 cups baby spinach, washed

Instructions:

1. Rinse the brown rice and add it to a pot with 2 cups of water. Bring to a boil, then reduce the heat to low and cover the pot. Cook for 25-30 minutes or until the rice is tender.
2. Heat the olive oil in a large pan over medium heat. Add the onion, garlic, and ginger and cook for 2-3 minutes until the onion is translucent.
3. Add the curry powder, turmeric, cumin, coriander, cinnamon, cardamom, and salt to the pan and stir to combine.
4. Add the red bell pepper and zucchini to the pan and cook for 5-7 minutes until they are slightly softened.
5. Add the diced tomatoes and lentils to the pan and stir to combine. Cook for 5-7 minutes until the mixture is heated through.
6. Serve the lentil curry over the brown rice with a side of steamed spinach.

Nutritional Values:

Calories: 330 kcal Fat: 6 g Carbohydrates: 56 g Fiber: 14 g Protein: 16 g Sodium: 680 mg

Seared Flank Steak

Preparation time: 15 minutes

Cooking Time: 30 minutes

Ingredients:

- 1 lb. flank steak
- 2 medium sweet potatoes peeled and chopped
- 1 lb. green beans, trimmed
- 4 cloves garlic, minced
- 2 sprigs fresh rosemary, chopped
- 1 tbsp. olive oil
- Salt and black pepper, to taste

Instructions:

1. Preheat the oven to 400°F.
2. In a mixing bowl, combine the sweet potatoes, garlic, rosemary, 1/2 tablespoon of olive oil, and a pinch of salt and black pepper.
3. Spread the sweet potato mixture in a single layer on a baking sheet and bake for 15-20 minutes, or until the sweet potatoes are tender.
4. While the sweet potatoes are cooking, heat a cast-iron skillet over high heat.
5. Rub the flank steak with the remaining olive oil and season it with salt and black pepper.

6. Once the skillet is hot, add the flank steak and cook for 3-4 minutes on each side, or until it's seared and browned on the outside and cooked to your desired level of doneness on the inside.

7. Remove the steak from the skillet and let it rest for a few minutes before slicing it thinly.

8. In the same skillet, add the green beans and cook for 2-3 minutes, or until they're tender but still crisp.

9. Serve the sliced steak with the roasted sweet potatoes and green beans on the side.

Nutritional Values:

Calories: 350 kcal Fat: 12 g Carbohydrates: 33 g Fiber: 8 g Protein: 30 g Sodium: 120 mg

---

Grilled Pork Chops

Preparation time: 20 minutes

Cooking Time: 35 minutes

Ingredients:

- 4 boneless pork chops
- 2 medium sweet potatoes, peeled and cut into 1-inch pieces
- 1 lb. Brussels sprouts trimmed and halved
- 1 teaspoon ground cumin

- 1 teaspoon smoked paprika
- 2 tablespoons olive oil
- Salt and black pepper to taste

Instructions:

1. Preheat the oven to 400°F (200°C).
2. In a large bowl, toss the sweet potatoes and Brussels sprouts with the cumin, paprika, olive oil, salt, and black pepper until evenly coated.
3. Arrange the vegetables in a single layer on a baking sheet and roast for 25 to 30 minutes, until tender and lightly browned, stirring halfway through.
4. While the vegetables are roasting, preheat a grill or grill pan over medium-high heat.
5. Season the pork chops with salt and black pepper to taste. Grill the pork chops for 5 to 6 minutes per side, until cooked through.
6. Serve the grilled pork chops with the roasted sweet potatoes and Brussels sprouts.

Nutritional Values:

Calories: 370 kcal Protein: 33 g Fat: 14 g Carbohydrates: 29 g Fiber: 8 g Sodium: 105 mg

Baked Salmon with Mixed Vegetables

Preparation time: 10 minutes

Cooking Time: 25 minutes

Servings: 4

Ingredients:

- 4 salmon fillets (4-6 oz each)
- 2 cups mixed vegetables (such as broccoli, bell peppers, zucchini)
- 2 cloves garlic, minced
- 1 tsp dried basil
- 1 tsp dried oregano
- 1/4 tsp black pepper
- 1/4 tsp salt
- 2 tbsp olive oil
- 2 cups cooked quinoa

Instructions:

1. Preheat the oven to 375°F (190°C).
2. In a bowl, combine the minced garlic, dried basil, dried oregano, black pepper, salt, and olive oil.
3. Place the salmon fillets in a baking dish and rub the garlic mixture over the fillets.
4. Place the mixed vegetables around the salmon fillets in the baking dish.

5. Bake in the preheated oven for 20-25 minutes, until the salmon is cooked through, and the vegetables are tender.

6. Serve the baked salmon and mixed vegetables with a side of cooked quinoa.

Nutritional Values:

Calories: 430 kcal Fat: 19 g Saturated Fat: 3 g Sodium: 236 mg Carbohydrates: 24 g Fiber: 4 g Sugar: 2 g Protein: 40 g Potassium: 1132 mg

Lemon and Herb Roasted Chicken

Preparation time: 10 minutes

Cooking Time: 1-hour

Servings: 4

Ingredients:

- 4 chicken thighs, skin-on
- 1 lemon juiced and zested
- 1 tablespoon olive oil
- 2 cloves garlic, minced
- 1 teaspoon dried thyme
- 2 teaspoon dried rosemary
- Salt and pepper, to taste
- 4 large carrots, peeled and sliced into 1-inch pieces
- 1 tablespoon honey

- 1 tablespoon balsamic vinegar
- 2 cups cooked brown rice

Instructions:

1. Preheat the oven to 375°F.
2. In a small bowl, combine the lemon juice, lemon zest, olive oil, garlic, thyme, and rosemary. Mix well.
3. Season the chicken thighs with salt and pepper, then rub the lemon and herb mixture all over the chicken.
4. Place the chicken thighs in a baking dish and roast for 40-45 minutes, until the skin is crispy, and the internal temperature of the chicken reaches 165°F.
5. While the chicken is cooking, prepare the roasted carrots. Toss the sliced carrots with honey, balsamic vinegar, and salt and pepper to taste. Spread the carrots in a single layer on a baking sheet and roast for 25-30 minutes, until tender and lightly caramelized.
6. Serve the roasted chicken with a side of roasted carrots and cooked brown rice.

Nutritional Values:

Calories: 395 Fat: 16g Carbohydrates: 34g Fiber: 5g Protein: 29g Sodium: 249mg

Black Bean and Vegetable Quesadillas

Preparation time: 15 minutes

Cooking Time: 15 minutes

Servings: 4

Ingredients:

- 1 can of black beans, drained and rinsed
- 1 red bell pepper, sliced
- 1 green bell pepper, sliced
- 1 onion, sliced
- 1 tbsp olive oil
- 1 tsp ground cumin
- 1 tsp smoked paprika
- 4 whole-grain tortillas
- 1/2 cup shredded cheddar cheese
- Salsa, to serve
- Mixed greens, to serve

Instructions:

1. Preheat the oven to 350°F (175°C).
2. In a large skillet, heat the olive oil over medium heat. Add the sliced onions and peppers, and sauté for 5-7 minutes until they are tender.
3. Add the black beans, cumin, and smoked paprika to the skillet, and stir until well combined. Cook for another 2-3 minutes until the black beans are heated through.

4. Lay the tortillas on a baking sheet. Divide the black bean and vegetable mixture evenly onto each tortilla, leaving a 1-inch border around the edge.
5. Sprinkle the shredded cheddar cheese over the black bean mixture on each tortilla.
6. Fold the tortillas in half, pressing down lightly.
7. Bake the quesadillas for 8-10 minutes until the cheese is melted and the tortillas are crispy.
8. Serve the quesadillas with salsa and mixed greens on the side.

Nutritional Values:

Calories: 340 kcal Fat: 13g Carbohydrates: 42g Fiber: 11g Protein: 16g Sodium: 370mg

---

Baked Turkey Meatballs

Preparation time: 15 minutes

Cooking Time: 25 minutes

Servings: 4

Ingredients:

For the meatballs:

- 1-pound ground turkey
- 1/2 cup breadcrumbs (preferably whole grain)
- 1 egg

- 1/4 cup chopped fresh parsley
- 1/4 cup grated Parmesan cheese
- 1/2 teaspoon garlic powder
- 1/2 teaspoon onion powder
- 1/2 teaspoon salt
- 1/4 teaspoon black pepper

For the tomato sauce:

- 1 can (28 ounces) crushed tomatoes
- 1 onion, chopped
- 3 garlic cloves, minced
- 1 tablespoon olive oil
- 1/2 teaspoon salt
- 1/4 teaspoon black pepper
- 1/4 teaspoon dried oregano
- 1/4 teaspoon dried basil

For the mixed vegetables:
- 2 cups mixed vegetables
- 1 tablespoon olive oil
- 1/2 teaspoon salt
- 1/4 teaspoon black pepper

For the whole-grain pasta:

- 8 ounces whole-grain pasta

Instructions:

1. Preheat the oven to 400°F.

2. In a large bowl, combine the ground turkey, breadcrumbs, egg, parsley, Parmesan cheese, garlic powder, onion powder, salt, and black pepper. Mix well.
3. Shape the mixture into 16 meatballs, each about 2 inches in diameter.
4. Place the meatballs on a baking sheet and bake for 15 minutes.
5. Meanwhile, make the tomato sauce. In a large skillet, heat the olive oil over medium heat. Add the onion and garlic and sauté until softened, about 5 minutes.
6. Add the crushed tomatoes, salt, black pepper, oregano, and basil to the skillet. Simmer for 10 minutes.
7. While the meatballs and tomato sauce are cooking, prepare the mixed vegetables. In a large bowl, toss the chopped vegetables with olive oil, salt, and black pepper.
8. Spread the vegetables on a separate baking sheet and roast in the oven for 15 minutes, until tender and lightly browned.
9. Cook the pasta according to package instructions.
10. Serve the meatballs with tomato sauce, mixed vegetables, and whole-grain pasta.

Nutritional Values:

Calories: 457 kcal Fat: 16 g Saturated Fat: 4 g Cholesterol: 115 mg Sodium:

1080 mg Carbohydrates: 47 g Fiber: 9 g Sugar: 12 g Protein: 34 g

Beef and Vegetable Stir-Fry

Preparation time: 15 minutes

Cooking Time: 15 minutes

Servings: 4

Ingredients:

- 1 lb. beef sirloin thinly sliced
- 2 tbsp cornstarch
- 2 tbsp low-sodium soy sauce
- 2 tbsp vegetable oil
- 2 cups broccoli florets
- 1 red bell pepper, sliced
- 1 yellow onion, sliced
- 2 garlic cloves, minced
- 1 tsp ginger, minced
- 1/4 cup beef broth
- Salt and black pepper, to taste
- 2 cups cooked brown rice

Instructions:

1. In a bowl, mix the beef, cornstarch, and soy sauce. Set aside.
2. Heat 1 tablespoon of vegetable oil in a large skillet over medium-high heat. Add the broccoli and stir-fry for 2-3 minutes until tender. Remove from the skillet and set aside.
3. Add the remaining tablespoon of vegetable oil to the skillet. Add the beef and stir-fry for 3-4 minutes until browned.

4. Add the red bell pepper, onion, garlic, and ginger to the skillet. Stir-fry for another 2-3 minutes until the vegetables are tender.

5. Pour the beef broth into the skillet and bring to a simmer. Stir to scrape any browned bits from the bottom of the skillet. Season with salt and black pepper, to taste.

6. Serve the beef and vegetable stir-fry with cooked brown rice and steamed broccoli on the side.

Nutritional Values:

Calories: 420 kcal Fat: 16g Carbohydrates: 34g Fiber: 5g Protein: 35g Sodium: 370mg

---

Spicy Shrimp and Vegetable Stir-Fry

Preparation time: 10 minutes

Cooking Time: 15 minutes

Servings: 4

Ingredients:

- 1-pound large shrimp, peeled and deveined
- 1 red bell pepper, sliced
- 1 yellow bell pepper, sliced
- 1 medium onion, sliced
- 2 cloves garlic, minced
- 1 tablespoon grated fresh ginger

- 1 tablespoon low-sodium soy sauce
- 2 teaspoons chili paste
- 1 teaspoon honey
- 2 tablespoons vegetable oil
- 1 cup brown rice
- 2 cups water
- Salt and black pepper, to taste
- 4 cups fresh spinach leaves washed and dried

Instructions:

1. Cook brown rice according to package directions.
2. Heat the vegetable oil in a large skillet over medium-high heat. Add the onion and cook until softened, about 2 minutes.
3. Add the garlic and ginger and cook for an additional minute.
4. Add the bell peppers and cook for 2-3 minutes until slightly softened.
5. In a small bowl, whisk together the soy sauce, chili paste, and honey.
6. Add the shrimp to the skillet and cook for 2-3 minutes, until pink and cooked through.
7. Pour the soy sauce mixture over the shrimp and vegetables and toss to coat.
8. Season with salt and black pepper, to taste.
9. Serve the stir-fry over the brown rice with a side of steamed spinach.

Nutritional Values:

Calories: 370 kcal Protein: 27g Fat: 10g Carbohydrates: 44g Fiber: 6g Sodium: 385mg

---

Turkey and Quinoa Stuffed Bell Peppers

Preparation time: 20 minutes

Cooking Time: 40 minutes

Servings: 4

Ingredients:

- 4 bell peppers halved and seeded
- 1-pound ground turkey
- 1 cup cooked quinoa
- 1 small onion, chopped
- 2 cloves garlic, minced
- 1 teaspoon dried oregano
- 1 teaspoon dried basil
- 1/2 teaspoon salt
- 1/4 teaspoon black pepper
- 1 cup low-sodium tomato sauce
- 1/4 cup shredded low-fat mozzarella cheese
- 1/4 cup chopped fresh parsley
- 1 bunch of asparagus trimmed and steamed

Instructions:

1. Preheat oven to 375°F.
2. In a large skillet, cook the ground turkey over medium-high heat until browned, stirring frequently to break up the meat.
3. Add the onion and garlic to the skillet and cook until the onion is translucent.
4. Add the cooked quinoa, oregano, basil, salt, and black pepper to the skillet and stir to combine.
5. Add the tomato sauce to the skillet and stir to combine. Cook until the mixture is heated through.
6. Spoon the turkey and quinoa mixture into the bell pepper halves and place them in a baking dish.
7. Cover the baking dish with foil and bake for 25 minutes.
8. Remove the foil from the baking dish, sprinkle the cheese on top of the stuffed peppers, and bake for an additional 10-15 minutes, or until the cheese is melted and the peppers are tender.
9. Serve with steamed asparagus on the side and garnish with chopped parsley.

Nutritional Values:

Calories: 290 Fat: 8g Saturated Fat: 2g Cholesterol: 60mg Sodium: 420mg

Carbohydrates: 24g Fiber: 6g Sugar: 9g Protein: 29g

Baked Chicken Parmesan

Preparation time: 20 minutes

Cooking Time: 45 minutes

Servings: 4

Ingredients:

- 4 boneless, skinless chicken breasts (about 1 1/2 pounds)
- 1/2 cup whole-wheat breadcrumbs
- 1/4 cup grated Parmesan cheese
- 1 teaspoon dried basil
- 1 teaspoon dried oregano
- 1/2 teaspoon garlic powder
- 1/2 teaspoon onion powder
- 1/4 teaspoon black pepper
- 1 egg, beaten
- 1 cup tomato sauce
- 4 ounces part-skim mozzarella cheese, shredded
- 8 ounces whole-grain pasta
- 2 medium zucchinis, sliced
- 1 tablespoon olive oil
- Salt and pepper, to taste

Instructions:

1. Preheat the oven to 375°F (190°C).

2. In a shallow dish, combine the breadcrumbs, Parmesan cheese, basil, oregano, garlic powder, onion powder, and black pepper.

3. In another shallow dish, beat the egg.

4. Dip each chicken breast first into the egg, and then into the breadcrumb mixture, coating both sides evenly.

5. Place the chicken breasts in a baking dish coated with cooking spray.

6. Bake for 25-30 minutes, or until the chicken is cooked through and the breadcrumbs are golden brown.

7. While the chicken is baking, cook the whole-grain pasta according to the package directions.

8. In a small saucepan, heat the tomato sauce over low heat.

9. In a separate baking dish, toss the sliced zucchini with olive oil, salt, and pepper.

10. After the chicken has baked for 25-30 minutes, add the shredded mozzarella cheese and tomato sauce on top of each chicken breast.

11. Return the chicken to the oven and bake for another 10-15 minutes, or until the cheese is melted and bubbly.

12. Meanwhile, roast the zucchini in the oven at 375°F (190°C) for 15-20 minutes, or until tender and lightly browned.

13. Serve the chicken with the whole-grain pasta and roasted zucchini on the side.

Nutritional Values:

Calories: 522 kcal Fat: 16 g Saturated Fat: 5 g Cholesterol: 160 mg Sodium: 792 mg Carbohydrates: 46 g Fiber: 8 g Sugar: 7 g Protein:

49 g Potassium: 926 mg

Shrimp and Vegetable Curry

Preparation time: 15 minutes

Cooking Time: 30 minutes

Servings: 4

- 1-pound medium shrimp, peeled and deveined
- 1 tablespoon olive oil
- 1 onion, chopped
- 2 garlic cloves, minced
- 1 tablespoon ginger, grated
- 2 teaspoons curry powder
- 1/2 teaspoon ground turmeric
- 1/2 teaspoon ground cumin
- 1/4 teaspoon cayenne pepper
- 1 can (14.5 oz) diced tomatoes, drained
- 1 can (14 oz) chickpeas rinsed and drained
- 1 large carrot, sliced
- 1 red bell pepper, chopped
- 1 cup low-sodium chicken broth
- Salt and black pepper to taste
- 2 cups cooked brown rice
- 1 head cauliflower, chopped

- 1 tablespoon olive oil
- 1/2 teaspoon salt

Instructions:

1. Preheat the oven to 425°F.
2. Toss the cauliflower with olive oil and salt on a baking sheet. Roast in the preheated oven for 20-25 minutes, or until tender and lightly browned.
3. Heat the olive oil in a large skillet over medium heat. Add the onion, garlic, and ginger, and sauté until soft, about 5 minutes.
4. Add the curry powder, turmeric, cumin, and cayenne pepper to the skillet, and cook for another 2 minutes, stirring frequently.
5. Add the tomatoes, chickpeas, carrot, red bell pepper, and chicken broth to the skillet. Bring to a boil, then reduce heat and simmer for 10-15 minutes, or until the vegetables are tender and the liquid has reduced slightly.
6. Add the shrimp to the skillet and cook until pink and opaque, about 3-5 minutes.
7. Serve the curry over the brown rice, with the roasted cauliflower on the side.

Nutritional Values:

Calories: 394 kcal Fat: 10 g Carbohydrates: 49 g Fiber: 12 g Protein: 30 g Sodium: 552 mg

Lemon and Herb Roasted Turkey Breast

Preparation time: 10 minutes

Cooking Time: 1 hour 30 minutes

Servings: 4

Ingredients:

- 1 (2 lb.) boneless turkey breast
- 2 tbsp olive oil
- 1 lemon juiced and zested
- 2 cloves garlic, minced
- 1 tsp dried thyme
- 1 tsp dried rosemary
- Salt and pepper, to taste
- 4 cups mixed vegetables (such as bell peppers, zucchini, onion, and carrots), chopped
- 2 cups cooked brown rice

Instructions:

1. Preheat oven to 375°F (190°C).
2. In a small bowl, whisk together the olive oil, lemon juice and zest, garlic, thyme, rosemary, salt, and pepper.
3. Rub the turkey breast with the lemon and herb mixture, making sure it is well coated.
4. Place the turkey breast in a baking dish and roast for 1 hour and 15 minutes or until the internal temperature reaches 165°F (74°C).

5. In a separate baking dish, toss the chopped vegetables with olive oil, salt, and pepper.

6. Roast the vegetables for 30 minutes or until they are tender and lightly browned.

7. Serve the turkey breast sliced with the roasted vegetables and brown rice.

Nutritional Values:

Calories: 470 kcal Fat: 14 g Carbohydrates: 39 g Fiber: 5 g Protein: 49 g Sodium: 315 mg

---

Seared Salmon with Roasted Brussels Sprouts

Preparation time: 10 minutes

Cooking Time: 25 minutes

Servings: 4

Ingredients:

- 4 salmon fillets (about 6 oz each), skin removed
- 1 lb. Brussels sprouts trimmed and halved
- 1 large, sweet potato, peeled and cut into 1-inch cubes
- 2 tbsp olive oil
- 1 tsp cumin
- 1 tsp paprika
- Salt and black pepper to taste

Instructions:

1. Preheat the oven to 400°F (200°C).
2. In a large bowl, toss the Brussels sprouts and sweet potato with olive oil, cumin, paprika, salt, and black pepper.
3. Arrange the vegetables in a single layer on a baking sheet and roast for 20-25 minutes, or until tender and browned.
4. Meanwhile, heat a non-stick skillet over medium-high heat. Season the salmon fillets with salt and black pepper.
5. Place the salmon fillets in the skillet, flesh side down, and cook for 3-4 minutes, or until golden brown.
6. Flip the salmon fillets over and cook for an additional 2-3 minutes, or until cooked through but still moist.
7. Serve the salmon fillets with the roasted Brussels sprouts and sweet potatoes.

Nutritional Values:

Calories: 390 kcal Fat: 20 g Carbohydrates: 19 g Fiber: 6 g Protein: 34 g Sodium: 175 mg

---

Grilled Chicken with Lemon and Herbs

Preparation time: 15 minutes

Cooking Time: 25 minutes

Servings: 4

Ingredients:

- 4 boneless, skinless chicken breasts
- 2 lemons juiced and zested
- 2 tablespoons olive oil
- 1 tablespoon dried oregano
- 1 tablespoon dried thyme
- Salt and pepper, to taste
- 2 medium sweet potatoes peeled and cubed
- 1-pound green beans, trimmed

Instructions:

1. Preheat the grill to medium-high heat.
2. In a small bowl, whisk together the lemon juice, lemon zest, olive oil, oregano, thyme, salt, and pepper to make the marinade.
3. Place the chicken breasts in a resealable plastic bag and pour the marinade over the chicken. Seal the bag and massage the chicken to coat it well with the marinade. Refrigerate for at least 30 minutes or up to 4 hours.
4. Meanwhile, preheat the oven to 400°F (200°C) and line a baking sheet with parchment paper.
5. Spread the sweet potatoes on the prepared baking sheet and drizzle with olive oil. Season with salt and pepper to taste. Roast for 20-25 minutes, until tender and lightly browned.

6. In a separate baking dish, spread out the green beans and toss with olive oil, salt, and pepper. Roast for 10-12 minutes, until tender and slightly charred.

7. Remove the chicken from the marinade and discard the remaining marinade. Grill the chicken for 6-8 minutes per side, or until cooked through and the juices run clear.

8. Serve the grilled chicken with a side of roasted sweet potatoes and green beans.

Nutritional Values:

Calories: 365kcal Fat: 12g Carbohydrates: 30g Fiber: 8g Protein: 38g Sodium: 190mg

---

Turkey and Vegetable Meatloaf

Preparation time: 20 minutes

Cooking Time: 1-hour

Servings: 6

Ingredients:

- 1 lb. ground turkey
- 1/2 cup whole-grain breadcrumbs
- 1/2 cup grated zucchini
- 1/2 cup grated carrots
- 1/4 cup diced onion
- 2 cloves garlic, minced

- 2 tablespoons chopped fresh parsley
- 1 tablespoon chopped fresh thyme
- 1 tablespoon Dijon mustard
- 1 egg, lightly beaten
- Salt and pepper, to taste
- 6-8 medium-sized carrots, peeled and sliced into sticks
- Mixed greens, for serving

Instructions:

1. Preheat the oven to 375°F (190°C). Line a baking sheet with parchment paper.
2. In a large bowl, mix the ground turkey, breadcrumbs, zucchini, carrots, onion, garlic, parsley, thyme, mustard, egg, salt, and pepper.
3. Shape the mixture into a loaf and place it on the prepared baking sheet.
4. Bake for 50-60 minutes, or until the internal temperature reaches 165°F (74°C).
5. While the meatloaf is cooking, toss the carrot sticks with salt and pepper and place them on another baking sheet. Roast for 20-25 minutes or until tender.
6. Serve the meatloaf with the roasted carrots and mixed greens on the side.

Nutritional Values:

Calories: 210 kcal Fat: 9g Carbohydrates: 15g Protein: 20g Sodium: 270mg Fiber: 3g

———◆———

Spicy Chicken and Vegetable Stir-Fry

Preparation time: 15 minutes

Cooking Time: 20 minutes

Servings: 4

Ingredients:

- 1-pound boneless, skinless chicken breast, cut into small pieces
- 1 tablespoon cornstarch
- 2 tablespoons low-sodium soy sauce
- 1 tablespoon honey
- 1 tablespoon vegetable oil
- 2 garlic cloves, minced
- 1 teaspoon grated ginger
- 1 small onion, chopped
- 1 red bell pepper, sliced
- 1 green bell pepper, sliced
- 1 cup sliced mushrooms
- 2 cups cooked brown rice
- 2 tablespoons chopped fresh cilantro
- 1 tablespoon sesame seeds
- 1/4 teaspoon red pepper flakes
- Salt and pepper, to taste

- 1-pound book choy trimmed and washed

Instructions:

1. In a bowl, whisk together cornstarch, soy sauce, honey, and 1/4 cup water until smooth.
2. In a large skillet or wok, heat oil over medium-high heat. Add garlic and ginger, and stirfry for 30 seconds.
3. Add chicken and onion to the skillet, and stir-fry until chicken is browned and cooked through, about 5-7 minutes.
4. Add red and green bell peppers and mushrooms, and stir-fry for 2-3 minutes until vegetables are slightly tender.
5. Pour in soy sauce mixture, and stir-fry for an additional 1-2 minutes until sauce thickens.
6. Stir in cilantro, sesame seeds, red pepper flakes, salt, and pepper.
7. In a separate pot, steam bok choy for 5-7 minutes until tender.
8. Serve stir-fry hot with brown rice and steamed bok choy on the side.

Nutritional Values:

Calories: 360 kcal Carbohydrates: 44 g Protein: 32 g Fat: 8 g Saturated Fat: 1 g Cholesterol: 66 mg Fiber: 7 g Sugar: 9 g Sodium: 437 mg

Poultry

Grilled Chicken Breasts

Preparation time: 10 minutes

Cooking Time: 20 minutes

Servings: 4

Ingredients:

- 4 boneless, skinless chicken breasts
- 1 large red bell pepper, sliced
- 1 large yellow onion, sliced
- 1 large zucchini, sliced
- 1 large yellow squash, sliced
- 1 tbsp olive oil
- 1 tbsp balsamic vinegar
- 1 tbsp dried Italian seasoning
- Salt and black pepper, to taste

Instructions:

1. Preheat the grill to medium-high heat.
2. Mix the sliced vegetables, olive oil, balsamic vinegar, Italian seasoning, salt, and black pepper in a large bowl.
3. Season the chicken breasts with salt and black pepper.
4. Place chicken breasts and vegetable mixture onto the grill. Grill chicken for 6-7 minutes per side or until fully cooked (internal temperature should reach 165°F). Grill vegetables for 8-10 minutes or until tender and lightly charred.

5. Remove chicken and vegetables from the grill and let rest for 5 minutes.

6. Serve chicken breasts with a side of mixed grilled vegetables.

Nutritional Values:

Calories: 235 Total fat: 8g Saturated fat: 1g Cholesterol: 74mg Sodium: 105mg Total carbohydrate: 11g Dietary fiber: 3g Sugars: 6g Protein: 31g

---

Baked Turkey Meatballs with Whole-Grain Pasta

Preparation time: 20 minutes

Cooking Time: 25 minutes

Servings: 4

Ingredients:

For the meatballs:

- 1 lb. lean ground turkey
- 1/2 cup whole-grain breadcrumbs
- 1 egg
- 2 tbsp grated Parmesan cheese
- 1 tbsp dried parsley
- 1/2 tsp garlic powder

- 1/2 tsp salt
- 1/4 tsp black pepper

For the pasta and sauce:

- 8 oz whole-grain spaghetti
- 2 cups low-sodium tomato sauce
- 1/2 tsp dried oregano
- 1/2 tsp dried basil
- 1/4 tsp red pepper flakes
- Salt and black pepper, to taste

Instructions:

1. Preheat oven to 400°F. Line a baking sheet with parchment paper.
2. Combine the ground turkey, breadcrumbs, egg, Parmesan cheese, parsley, garlic powder, salt, and black pepper in a large bowl. Mix until well combined.
3. Place the mixture into a 1 1/2-inch meatball on the prepared baking sheet.
4. Bake the meatballs for 20-25 minutes or until fully cooked (internal temperature should reach 165°F).
5. While the meatballs are baking, cook the whole-grain spaghetti according to the package instructions.
6. In a saucepan, heat the tomato sauce over medium heat. Add the oregano, basil, red pepper flakes, salt, and black pepper. Simmer for 5-10 minutes or until heated through.
7. Serve the meatballs over the whole-grain spaghetti, topped with tomato sauce.

Nutritional Values:

Calories: 426 Total fat: 11g Saturated fat: 3g Cholesterol: 128mg
Sodium: 577mg Total carbohydrate: 46g Dietary fiber: 8g Sugars: 9g
Protein: 38g

Grilled Chicken with Lemon and Herbs

Preparation time: 15 minutes

Cooking Time: 35 minutes

Servings: 4

Ingredients:

For the chicken:

- 4 boneless, skinless chicken breasts
- 2 tbsp olive oil
- 1 tbsp dried basil
- 1 tbsp dried thyme
- 1 tbsp dried oregano
- 1 lemon, juiced
- Salt and black pepper, to taste

For the sweet potatoes and green beans:

- 2 large, sweet potatoes, peeled and diced
- 1 lb. fresh green beans, trimmed
- 2 tbsp olive oil

- 1 tsp garlic powder
- 1 tsp paprika
- Salt and black pepper, to taste

Instructions:

1. Preheat the grill to medium-high heat.
2. Mix the olive oil, dried herbs, lemon juice, salt, and black pepper in a small bowl. Brush the chicken breasts with the mixture.
3. Place the chicken breasts onto the grill. Grill for 6-7 minutes per side or until fully cooked (internal temperature should reach 165°F).
4. While the chicken is grilling, preheat the oven to 425°F. Line a baking sheet with parchment paper.
5. Toss the diced sweet potatoes, green beans, olive oil, garlic powder, paprika, salt, and black pepper in a large bowl. Spread the mixture onto the prepared baking sheet.
6. Roast the sweet potatoes and green beans for 20-25 minutes or until tender and lightly browned.
7. Serve the grilled chicken breasts with roasted sweet potatoes and green beans.

Nutritional Values:

Calories: 406 Total fat: 17g Saturated fat: 3g Cholesterol: 96mg
Sodium: 143mg Total carbohydrate: 28g Dietary fiber: 7g Sugars: 8g
Protein: 38g

Baked Chicken Thighs

Preparation time: 15 minutes

Cooking Time: 45 minutes

Servings: 4

Ingredients:

For the chicken:

- 4 bone-in, skin-on chicken thighs
- 1 tbsp olive oil
- 1 tsp garlic powder
- 1 tsp dried thyme
- Salt and black pepper, to taste

For the Brussels sprouts and carrots:

- 1 lb. Brussels sprouts trimmed and halved
- 4 large carrots peeled and sliced
- 1 tbsp olive oil
- 1 tsp garlic powder
- 1 tsp dried thyme
- Salt and black pepper, to taste

Instructions:

1. Preheat oven to 375°F. Line a baking sheet with parchment paper.
2. Mix the olive oil, garlic powder, dried thyme, salt, and black pepper in a small bowl.

3. Brush the chicken thighs with the mixture.

4. Place the chicken thighs onto the prepared baking sheet.

5. Toss the halved Brussels sprouts, sliced carrots, olive oil, garlic powder, dried thyme, salt, and black pepper in a large bowl. Spread the mixture onto the prepared baking sheet around the chicken thighs.

6. Bake for 40-45 minutes until the chicken is fully cooked (internal temperature should reach 165°F) and the vegetables are tender and lightly browned.

7. Serve the baked chicken thighs with roasted Brussels sprouts and carrots.

Nutritional Values:

Calories: 364 Total fat: 19g Saturated fat: 4g Cholesterol: 113mg Sodium:

184mg Total carbohydrate: 20g Dietary fiber: 7g Sugars: 7g Protein: 29g

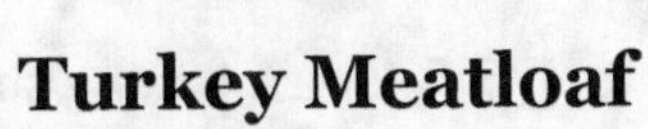

Turkey Meatloaf

Preparation time: 15 minutes

Cooking Time: 1-hour

Servings: 6

Ingredients:

For the meatloaf:

- 2 lbs. ground turkey
- 1/2 cup whole-grain breadcrumbs
- 1/2 cup unsweetened almond milk
- 2 eggs
- 1 small onion finely chopped
- 1 tbsp dried rosemary
- 1 tsp garlic powder
- 1 tsp salt
- 1/2 tsp black pepper
- 1/2 cup low-sodium tomato sauce

For the cauliflower and carrots:

- 1 head cauliflower, cut into florets
- 4 large carrots peeled and sliced
- 2 tbsp olive oil
- 1 tbsp dried rosemary
- Salt and black pepper, to taste

Instructions:

1. Preheat oven to 375°F. Line a baking sheet with parchment paper.
2. Combine the ground turkey, breadcrumbs, almond milk, eggs, onion, dried rosemary, garlic powder, salt, and black pepper in a large bowl. Mix until well combined.
3. Transfer the mixture to a loaf pan. Spread the tomato sauce over the top of the meatloaf.
4. Bake the meatloaf for 50-60 minutes or until fully cooked (internal temperature should reach 165°F).

5. While the meatloaf is baking, preheat the oven to 425°F. Line a baking sheet with parchment paper.

6. Toss the cauliflower florets, sliced carrots, olive oil, dried rosemary, salt, and black pepper in a large bowl. Spread the mixture onto the prepared baking sheet.

7. Roast the cauliflower and carrots for 20-25 minutes or until tender and lightly browned.

8. Serve the turkey meatloaf with a side of roasted cauliflower and carrots.

Nutritional Values:

Calories: 357 Total fat: 15g Saturated fat: 4g Cholesterol: 181mg Sodium: 662mg Total carbohydrate: 21g Dietary fiber: 6g Sugars: 6g Protein: 36g

Chicken and Vegetable Fajita Bowl with Quinoa

Preparation time: 15 minutes

Cooking Time: 25 minutes

Servings: 4

Ingredients:

For the chicken and vegetables:

- 1 lb. boneless, skinless chicken breast sliced into thin strips
- 2 bell peppers, seeded and cut into thin strips
- 1 large onion, cut into thin strips

- 2 tbsp olive oil
- 1 tbsp chili powder
- 1 tsp ground cumin
- 1/2 tsp garlic powder
- Salt and black pepper, to taste

For the quinoa:

- 1 cup quinoa, rinsed
- 2 cups water
- 1/2 tsp salt

For the mixed greens:
- 4 cups mixed greens
- 2 tbsp balsamic vinegar
- 1 tbsp olive oil

Instructions:

1. Preheat oven to 400°F. Line a baking sheet with parchment paper.
2. In a large bowl, toss together the chicken strips, sliced bell peppers, sliced onion, olive oil, chili powder, ground cumin, garlic powder, salt, and black pepper.
3. Spread the mixture onto the prepared baking sheet.
4. Bake for 20-25 minutes until the chicken is fully cooked and the vegetables are tender and lightly browned.
5. While the chicken and vegetables are baking, prepare the quinoa. Bring the rinsed quinoa, water, and salt to a boil in a medium saucepan. Reduce heat to low, cover, and simmer

for 15-20 minutes or until the water is fully absorbed and the quinoa is tender.

6. Toss the mixed greens, balsamic vinegar, and olive oil in a large bowl.

7. Divide the quinoa among 4 bowls. Top each bowl with the chicken and vegetable mixture and mixed greens.

Nutritional Values:

Calories: 375 Total fat: 14g Saturated fat: 2g Cholesterol: 74mg Sodium: 398mg Total carbohydrate: 36g Dietary fiber: 7g Sugars: 7g Protein: 29g

Grilled Chicken Caesar Salad

Preparation time: 20 minutes

Cooking Time: 20 minutes

Servings: 2

Ingredients:

For the chicken:

- 4 boneless, skinless chicken breasts
- 1 tbsp olive oil
- 1 tsp garlic powder
- Salt and black pepper, to taste

For the salad:

- 8 cups chopped romaine lettuce
- 1/2 cup freshly grated Parmesan cheese
- 1/2 cup whole-grain croutons
- 1/4 cup chopped fresh parsley

<u>For the dressing:</u>

- 1/2 cup plain Greek yogurt
- 2tbsp freshly squeezed lemon juice
- 2 tbsp Dijon mustard
- 2 tbsp grated Parmesan cheese
- 1 tbsp Worcestershire sauce
- 1 tsp garlic powder
- Salt and black pepper, to taste

<u>For the bread:</u>

- 4 slices whole-grain bread
- 1 tbsp olive oil
- 1 tsp garlic powder

Instructions:

1. Preheat the grill to medium-high heat.

2. Brush the chicken breasts with olive oil and season with garlic powder, salt, and black pepper.

    1. Grill the chicken for 6-7 minutes per side or until fully cooked (internal temperature should reach 165°F). Set aside.

2. Combine the chopped romaine lettuce, freshly grated Parmesan cheese, whole-grain croutons, and chopped fresh parsley in a large bowl.

3. Whisk together the plain Greek yogurt, freshly squeezed lemon juice, Dijon mustard, grated Parmesan cheese, Worcestershire sauce, garlic powder, salt, and black pepper in a small bowl.

4. Heat a non-stick skillet over medium heat. Brush the slices of whole-grain bread with olive oil and sprinkle with garlic powder. Toast the bread in the skillet until lightly browned on both sides.

5. Divide the salad among 4 plates. Top each dish with grilled chicken breast and drizzle with the homemade dressing. Serve with a slice of whole-grain bread on the side.

Nutritional Values:

Calories: 401 Total fat: 16g Saturated fat: 4g Cholesterol: 99mg Sodium: 697mg Total carbohydrate: 29g Dietary fiber: 5g Sugars: 5g Protein: 36g

Chicken and Vegetable Lettuce Wraps

Preparation time: 20 minutes

Cooking Time: 10 minutes

Servings: 2

Ingredients:

For the chicken and vegetables:

- 1 lb. ground chicken
- 1 tbsp olive oil
- 1 red bell pepper seeded and diced
- 1 cup chopped mushrooms
- 1 cup shredded carrots
- 2 green onions, chopped
- 2 cloves garlic, minced
- Salt and black pepper, to taste
- 8 large lettuce leaves

For the peanut sauce:

- 1/4 cup natural peanut butter
- 2 tbsp low-sodium soy sauce
- 2 tbsp rice vinegar
- 1 tbsp honey
- 1 tbsp sesame oil
- 1 tbsp water
- 1/2 tsp garlic powder
- Pinch of red pepper flakes

Instructions:

1. Heat olive oil in a large skillet over medium-high heat. Add the ground chicken, red bell pepper, mushrooms, shredded carrots, green onions, and minced garlic. Cook for 7-10 minutes or until the chicken is fully cooked and the vegetables are tender.

2. Whisk together the peanut butter, low-sodium soy sauce, rice vinegar, honey, sesame oil, water, garlic powder, and red pepper flakes in a small bowl.

3. To assemble the lettuce wraps, spoon the chicken and vegetable mixture onto each lettuce leaf. Drizzle with the peanut sauce and serve.

Nutritional Values:

Calories: 302 Total fat: 19g Saturated fat: 4g Cholesterol: 98mg Sodium: 478mg Total carbohydrate: 12g Dietary fiber: 3g Sugars: 6g Protein: 25g

Grilled Chicken and Vegetable Wrap

Preparation time: 20 minutes

Cooking Time: 15 minutes

Servings: 4

Ingredients:

For the chicken and vegetables:

- 1 lb. boneless, skinless chicken breasts
- 1 tbsp olive oil
- 1 red bell pepper seeded and sliced
- 1 yellow squash, sliced
- 1 zucchini, sliced
- 1 red onion, sliced

- Salt and black pepper, to taste

<u>For the wrap:</u>

- 4 whole-wheat tortillas
- 1/2 cup hummus
- 1/4 cup crumbled feta cheese
- 1/4 cup chopped fresh parsley
- Juice of 1/2 lemon

Instructions:

1. Preheat the grill to medium-high heat.
2. Brush the chicken breasts with olive oil and season with salt and black pepper.
3. Grill the chicken for 6-7 minutes per side or until fully cooked (internal temperature should reach 165°F). Set aside.
4. Toss the sliced red bell pepper, yellow squash, zucchini, and red onion with olive oil, salt, and black pepper in a large bowl. Grill for 5-7 minutes or until tender and slightly charred. Set aside.
5. To assemble the wrap, spread 2 tablespoons of hummus onto each tortilla. Top with sliced grilled chicken, grilled vegetables, crumbled feta cheese, chopped fresh parsley, and a squeeze of fresh lemon juice.
6. Roll up the tortilla and cut it in half diagonally. Serve immediately.

Nutritional Values:

Calories: 375 Total fat: 15g Saturated fat: 4g Cholesterol: 74mg Sodium: 604mg Total carbohydrate: 31g Dietary fiber: 7g Sugars: 5g Protein: 30g

Spicy Chicken and Vegetable Stir-Fry

Preparation time: 20 minutes

Cooking Time: 20 minutes

Servings:

Ingredients:

<u>For the stir-fry:</u>

- 1 lb. boneless, skinless chicken breasts cut into small pieces
- 2 tbsp low-sodium soy sauce
- 2 tbsp rice vinegar
- 1 tbsp cornstarch
- 1 tbsp sesame oil
- 2 cloves garlic, minced
- 1 tbsp grated fresh ginger
- 1 red bell pepper seeded and sliced
- 1 yellow bell pepper seeded and sliced
- 1 cup sliced mushrooms
- 1 cup sliced zucchini
- 2 green onions, chopped
- Salt and black pepper, to taste

For the brown rice:

- 1 cup brown rice
- 2 cups water
- Pinch of salt

Instructions:

1. Whisk together the low-sodium soy sauce, rice vinegar, cornstarch, and sesame oil in a small bowl. Set aside.
2. Cook the brown rice according to package instructions with a pinch of salt.
3. Heat a large skillet or wok over high heat. Add the minced garlic and grated ginger and cook for 30 seconds or until fragrant.
4. Add the chicken and cook for 5-7 minutes or until fully cooked.
5. Add the sliced bell peppers, mushrooms, and zucchini to the skillet and cook for 3-4 minutes or until tender.
6. Pour the soy sauce mixture over the chicken and vegetables and stir to coat evenly. Cook for 1-2 minutes or until the sauce thickens.
7. Serve the stir-fry over brown rice and sprinkle with chopped green onions.

Nutritional Values:

Calories: 344 Total fat: 7g Saturated fat: 1g Cholesterol: 73mg Sodium: 455mg Total carbohydrate: 39g Dietary fiber: 5g Sugars: 5g Protein: 32g

Baked Chicken and Vegetable Egg Cups

Preparation time: 15 minutes

Cooking Time: 25 minutes

Servings: 6

Ingredients:

- 1 lb. boneless, skinless chicken breasts cut into small pieces
- 1 red bell pepper seeded and diced
- 1 zucchini, diced
- 1/2 red onion, diced
- 1/2 cup chopped fresh parsley
- 8 eggs
- 1/2 cup of low-fat milk
- 1/2 tsp salt
- 1/4 tsp black pepper
- Cooking spray

Instructions:

1. Preheat oven to 375°F. Spray a 12-cup muffin tin with cooking spray.
2. In a large bowl, combine the chicken, diced red bell pepper, zucchini, red onion, and chopped fresh parsley.
3. Whisk together the eggs, low-fat milk, salt, and black pepper in a separate bowl.
4. Add the egg mixture to the chicken and vegetable mixture and stir to combine.
5. Divide the mixture evenly among the 12 muffin cups.

6. Bake for 20-25 minutes or until the egg cups are set and golden brown.

7. Let cool for a few minutes before removing it from the muffin tin. Serve warm or at room temperature.

Nutritional Values:

Calories: 180 Total fat: 6g Saturated fat: 2g Cholesterol: 298mg Sodium: 330mg Total carbohydrate: 5g Dietary fiber: 1g Sugars: 3g Protein: 25g

---

Turkey Chili with Beans and Diced Vegetables

Preparation time: 15 minutes

Cooking Time: 40 minutes

Servings: 6

Ingredients:

- 1-pound ground turkey
- 1 tablespoon olive oil
- 1 onion, chopped
- 1 bell peppers, chopped
- 2 cloves garlic, minced
- 1 can (14.5 oz) diced tomatoes
- 1 can (15 oz) kidney beans, drained and rinsed
- 1 can (15 oz) black beans, drained and rinsed

- 1 cup chicken broth
- 2 tablespoons chili powder
- 1 teaspoon ground cumin
- Salt and pepper to taste
- Whole-grain bread for serving

Instructions:

1. Preheat a large pot or Dutch oven over medium-high heat. Add the olive oil and ground turkey, breaking it up with a wooden spoon as it cooks.
2. Once the turkey is browned and cooked through, add the chopped onion, bell peppers, and minced garlic. Cook until the vegetables are soft, and the onion is translucent about 5 minutes.
3. Add the diced tomatoes (with their juice), kidney beans, black beans, chicken broth, chili powder, cumin, salt, and pepper. Stir to combine.
4. Bring the mixture to a boil, then reduce the heat and simmer for 25-30 minutes, until the chili is thick, and the vegetables are tender.
5. Serve hot with whole-grain bread on the side.

Nutritional Values:

Calories: 314 kcal Fat: 11 g Carbohydrates: 29 g Fiber: 10 g Protein: 26 g Sodium: 657 mg

Vegetables

Roasted Asparagus with Lemon and Garlic

Preparation time: 5 minutes

Cooking Time: 15 minutes

Servings: 4

Ingredients:

- 1-pound fresh asparagus, trimmed
- 2 tablespoons olive oil
- 2 cloves garlic, minced
- lemon juiced and zested
- Salt and pepper to taste

Instructions:

1. Preheat the oven to 400°F (200°C).
2. Arrange the asparagus in a single layer on a baking sheet.
3. Drizzle the olive oil over the asparagus and toss to coat evenly.
4. Sprinkle the garlic, lemon zest, and lemon juice over the asparagus and toss to coat.
5. Season with salt and pepper to taste.
6. Roast in the oven for 12-15 minutes or until the asparagus is tender but slightly crisp.
7. Serve hot as a side dish.

Nutritional Values:

Calories: 76 kcal Fat: 7g Carbohydrates: 4g Fiber: 2g Protein: 2g Sodium: 2mg

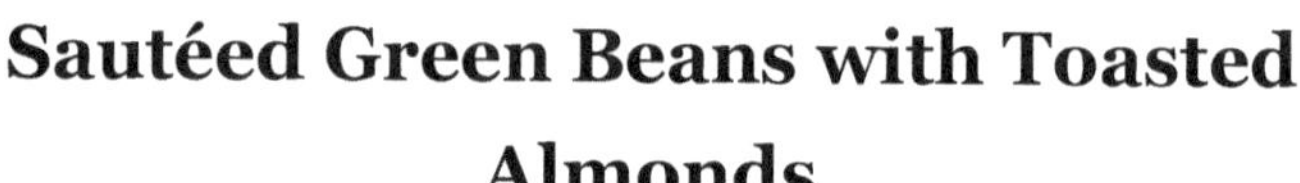

Sautéed Green Beans with Toasted Almonds

Preparation time: 10 minutes

Cooking Time: 15 minutes

Servings: 4

Ingredients:

- 1 lb. green beans, trimmed
- 2 tbsp olive oil
- 2 cloves garlic, minced
- 1/4 cup slivered almonds
- Salt and pepper, to taste

Instructions:

1. Heat the olive oil in a large skillet over medium heat.
2. Add the green beans to the skillet and sauté for 5-7 minutes or until they soften.
3. Add the garlic to the skillet and sauté for 1-2 minutes or until fragrant.

4. Add the slivered almonds to the skillet and sauté for 2-3 minutes, until they are toasted and golden brown.

5. Season with salt and pepper to taste.

6. Serve hot and enjoy!

Nutritional Values:

Calories: 110 kcal Fat: 9 g Carbohydrates: 7 g Protein: 2 g Sodium: 150 mg Fiber: 3 g

Steamed Broccoli

Preparation time: 5 minutes

Cooking Time: 10 minutes

Servings: 4

Ingredients:

- 1-pound broccoli florets
- 2 garlic cloves, minced
- 1 lemon juiced and zested
- 2 tablespoons olive oil
- Salt and pepper, to taste

Instructions:

1. Rinse the broccoli florets under running water and place them in a steamer basket.

2. Add water to a pot and bring it to a boil. Once boiling, place the steamer basket with the broccoli over the pool and cover it with a lid.
3. Steam the broccoli for about 8-10 minutes or until tender but still crisp.
4. While the broccoli is steaming, heat the olive oil in a pan over medium heat.
5. Add the minced garlic to the pan and sauté for 1-2 minutes or until fragrant.
6. Remove the pan from the heat and add the lemon juice and zest to the pan. Mix well.
7. Once the broccoli is steamed, transfer it to a large bowl and pour the lemon-garlic mixture over the top.
8. Toss the broccoli until it is well coated with the mixture.
9. Season with salt and pepper to taste.
10. Serve warm.

Nutritional Values:

Calories: 84 kcal Fat: 6.7 g Carbohydrates: 7.4 g Fiber: 2.9 g Protein: 3.3 g Sodium: 36 mg

---

Balsamic Roasted Carrots

Preparation time: 10 minutes

Cooking Time: 25 minutes

Servings: 4

- 1-pound carrots, peeled and sliced into 1-inch pieces
- 1 tablespoon olive oil
- 1 tablespoon balsamic vinegar
- 2 cloves garlic, minced
- 1 teaspoon dried thyme
- 1 teaspoon dried rosemary
- 1/2 teaspoon salt
- 1/4 teaspoon black pepper

Instructions:

1. Preheat the oven to 400°F (200°C).
2. Mix the olive oil, balsamic vinegar, garlic, thyme, rosemary, salt, and black pepper in a large bowl.
3. Add the sliced carrots to the bowl and toss to coat with the herb mixture.
4. Spread the carrots in a single layer on a baking sheet lined with parchment paper.
5. Roast the carrots for 20-25 minutes or until tender and lightly browned.
6. Serve hot as a side dish.

Nutritional Values:

Calories: 85kcal Fat: 4g Carbohydrates: 13g Fiber: 4g Protein: 1g Sodium: 350mg

Garlic Roasted Cherry Tomatoes

Preparation time: 5 minutes

Cooking Time: 15-20 minutes

Servings: 4

Ingredients:

- 2 cups cherry tomatoes
- 2 garlic cloves, minced
- 1 tablespoon olive oil
- 1/4 teaspoon salt
- 1/8 teaspoon black pepper
- 1 tablespoon chopped fresh basil

Instructions:

1. Preheat the oven to 400°F (200°C).
2. Mix the minced garlic, olive oil, salt, and black pepper in a small bowl.
3. Place the cherry tomatoes in a baking dish, drizzle the garlic and oil mixture over them, and toss to coat.
4. Roast the cherry tomatoes for 15-20 minutes until they wrinkle and burst.
5. Remove from the oven and sprinkle with chopped fresh basil before serving.

Nutritional Values:

Calories: 48kcal Fat: 3g Saturated Fat: 0g Cholesterol: 0mg

Sodium: 150mg Potassium: 206mg Carbohydrates: 4g Fiber: 1g Sugar: 2g Protein: 1g

Grilled Eggplant with Balsamic Glaze

Preparation time: 10 minutes

Cooking Time: 10 minutes

Servings: 4

Ingredients:

- 2 medium eggplants, sliced into rounds
- 1/4 cup balsamic vinegar
- 2 tablespoons olive oil
- 2 garlic cloves, minced
- Salt and pepper, to taste
- 1/4 cup fresh parsley, chopped

Instructions:

1. Preheat the grill to medium-high heat.
2. Whisk together balsamic vinegar, olive oil, garlic, salt, and pepper in a small bowl.
3. Brush both sides of the eggplant slices with the balsamic mixture.
4. Place eggplant slices on the grill and cook for 4-5 minutes per side or until tender and slightly charred.

5. Remove eggplant from the grill and sprinkle with fresh parsley.

6. Serve immediately.

Nutritional Values:

Calories: 109 Fat: 7g Protein: 2g Carbohydrates: 12g Fiber: 6g Sodium: 6mg

---

Spicy Roasted Cauliflower

Preparation time: 10 minutes

Cooking Time: 20 minutes

Servings: 4

Ingredients:

- 1 large head of cauliflower, cut into bite-sized florets
- 2 tbsp olive oil
- 3 cloves garlic, minced
- 1 tsp dried oregano
- 1/2 tsp dried thyme
- 1/2 tsp smoked paprika
- 1/4 tsp cayenne pepper (adjust to taste)
- Salt and pepper, to taste
- Fresh parsley, chopped, for garnish

Instructions:

1. Preheat the oven to 425°F (220°C).
2. Combine the cauliflower florets, olive oil, minced garlic, oregano, thyme, smoked paprika, cayenne pepper, salt, and pepper in a large bowl. Toss well to coat evenly.
3. Spread the cauliflower mixture in a single layer on a baking sheet.
4. Roast in the oven for 15-20 minutes or until the cauliflower is tender and golden brown.
5. Remove from the oven and let cool for a few minutes. Garnish with chopped fresh parsley before serving.

Nutritional Values:

Calories: 92 kcal Fat: 7 g Carbohydrates: 7 g Fiber: 3 g Protein: 3 g Sodium: 17 mg

Roasted Butternut Squash with Maple Syrup

Preparation time: 15 minutes

Cooking Time: 40 minutes

Servings: 4

Ingredients:

- 1 medium butternut squash, peeled, seeded, and cubed
- 1 tablespoon olive oil
- 1 tablespoon maple syrup

- 1 teaspoon ground cinnamon
- Salt and black pepper, to taste

Instructions:

1. Preheat the oven to 400°F (200°C).
2. Mix the butternut squash cubes with olive oil, maple syrup, cinnamon, salt, and black pepper in a bowl.
3. Spread the mixture on a baking sheet and roast in the oven for 40 minutes or until the squash is tender and lightly browned.
4. Serve hot.

Nutritional Values:

Calories: 108 kcal Fat: 3 g Carbohydrates: 22 g Fiber: 4 g Protein: 2 g Sodium: 85 mg

Sauteed Spinach with Garlic and Lemon

Preparation time: 5 minutes

Cooking Time: 5 minutes

Servings: 4

Ingredients:

- 1 lb. fresh spinach washed and trimmed
- 2 tbsp olive oil
- 3 cloves garlic, minced

- 1/2 tsp salt
- 1/4 tsp black pepper
- Juice of 1 lemon

Instructions:

1. Heat the olive oil in a large skillet over medium heat.
2. Add the minced garlic and sauté for 1-2 minutes until fragrant.
3. Add the spinach to the skillet and toss with the garlic until wilted, about 2-3 minutes.
4. Season with salt and black pepper to taste.
5. Squeeze the juice of 1 lemon over the spinach and toss to combine.
6. Serve hot and enjoy!

Nutritional Values:

Calories: 81 kcal Fat: 7 g Carbohydrates: 4 g Protein: 3 g Sodium: 328 mg Potassium: 551 mg Fiber: 2 g Vitamin A: 116% Vitamin C: 45% Calcium: 10% Iron: 18%

Steamed Beets with Goat Cheese

Preparation time: 10 minutes

Cooking Time: 35-40 minutes

Servings: 4

Ingredients:

- 4 medium beets trimmed and washed

- 2 oz goat cheese, crumbled
- 1/4 cup walnuts, chopped
- 1 tbsp olive oil
- Salt and pepper to taste

Instructions:

1. Preheat the oven to 400°F (200°C).
2. If roasting, wrap the beets in aluminum foil and place them on a baking sheet. If steaming, place the beets in a steamer basket.
3. Roast the beets for 35-40 minutes or until tender. If steaming, cook for 20-25 minutes or until tender.
4. Let the beets cool until they can be handled, then peel off the skin and slice them into rounds.
5. Whisk together the olive oil, salt, and pepper in a small bowl.
6. Arrange the beet slices on a plate, crumble goat cheese on top, sprinkle with chopped walnuts, and drizzle with olive oil.
7. Serve warm or at room temperature.

Nutritional Values:

Calories: 140 Fat: 9g Carbohydrates: 10g Fiber: 3g Protein: 6g Sodium: 160mg

Garlic Roasted Bell Peppers

Preparation time: 10 minutes

Cooking Time: 25 minutes

Ingredients:

- 4 bell peppers (red, yellow, or orange)
- 2 tablespoons olive oil
- 3 cloves garlic, minced
- Salt and pepper to taste

Instructions:

1. Preheat the oven to 400°F (200°C).
2. Cut the bell peppers into quarters and remove the seeds and stems.
3. Mix the olive oil, garlic, salt, and pepper in a small bowl.
4. Place the bell pepper quarters on a baking sheet lined with parchment paper.
5. Brush the bell pepper quarters with the olive oil, coating them evenly.
6. Roast the bell peppers in the oven for 25 minutes or until tender and lightly browned.
7. Remove from the oven and let cool for a few minutes before serving.

Nutritional Values:

Calories: 94 kcal Protein: 2 g Fat: 7 g Carbohydrates: 8 g Fiber: 2 g Sodium: 14 mg

Stir-Fried Mixed Vegetables

Preparation time: 10 minutes

Cooking Time: 10 minutes

Ingredients:

- 1 tablespoon olive oil
- 1 red bell pepper, sliced
- 1 green bell pepper, sliced
- 1 zucchini, sliced
- 1 yellow squash, sliced
- 1 cup snow peas
- 1 tablespoon fresh ginger, grated
- 2 cloves garlic, minced
- 2 tablespoons low-sodium soy sauce
- 1 tablespoon rice vinegar
- 1 teaspoon honey
- Salt and pepper, to taste
- 2 tablespoons green onions, chopped (optional)

Instructions:

1. Heat the olive oil in a large skillet over medium-high heat.
2. Add the sliced bell peppers, zucchini, and yellow squash to the skillet and stir-fry for 2-3 minutes.
3. Add the snow peas, ginger, and garlic to the skillet and stir-fry for 2-3 minutes.

4. Whisk together the soy sauce, rice vinegar, honey, salt, and pepper in a small bowl.

5. Pour the soy sauce mixture over the vegetables and stir to coat evenly. Cook for an additional 1-2 minutes, until the vegetables are tender, and the sauce has thickened slightly.

6. Remove the skillet from heat and sprinkle with chopped green onions, if desired.

7. Serve immediately over brown rice or quinoa, if desired.

Nutritional Values:

Calories: 87kcal Fat: 4g Carbohydrates: 11g Protein: 3g Sodium: 318mg Fiber: 3g

Roasted Acorn Squash

Preparation time: 10 minutes

Cooking Time: 40 minutes

Ingredients:

- 2 small acorn squashes halved and seeded
- 2 tbsp. olive oil
- 1 tbsp. honey
- 1 tbsp. fresh thyme leaves
- 1/2 tsp. salt
- 1/4 tsp. black pepper

Instructions:

1. Preheat the oven to 400°F (200°C).
2. Cut each acorn squash in half and remove the seeds.
3. Whisk together olive oil, honey, thyme leaves, salt, and black pepper in a small bowl.
4. Brush the honey mixture over each acorn squash half.
5. Place the squash halves on a baking sheet, cut side down, and roast for 20 minutes.
6. Flip the squash halves over and continue roasting for 20 minutes until tender and golden brown.
7. Serve hot.

Nutritional Values:

Calories: 140 kcal Fat: 8 g Carbohydrates: 18 g Fiber: 2.5 g Protein: 1.5 g Sodium: 300 mg

---

Grilled Corn on The Cob

Preparation time: 10 minutes

Cooking Time: 15 minutes

Ingredients:

- 4 ears of corn, husks removed
- 2 tablespoons olive oil
- 1/2 teaspoon salt
- 1/4 teaspoon black pepper
- 2 tablespoons unsalted butter at room temperature
- 1 clove garlic, minced

- 1 tablespoon chopped fresh herbs (such as parsley, thyme, or chives)

Instructions:

1. Preheat the grill to medium-high heat.
2. Brush the corn with olive oil and sprinkle with salt and pepper.
3. Grill the corn, turning occasionally, until tender and charred in spots, about 10-12 minutes.
4. While the corn is grilling, mix the butter, garlic, and herbs in a small bowl.
5. When the corn is done, spread the butter mixture evenly over each ear of corn.
6. Serve hot and enjoy!

Nutritional Values:

Calories: 165 Fat: 10g Carbohydrates: 21g Fiber: 3g Protein: 3g Sodium: 305mg

Cucumber Salad with Red Onion

Preparation time: 10 minutes.

Servings: 4

Ingredients:

- 2 large cucumbers peeled and sliced
- 1 small red onion thinly sliced

- 1/4 cup chopped fresh dill
- 2 tbsp olive oil
- 2 tbsp red wine vinegar
- 1 tsp Dijon mustard
- Salt and pepper to taste

Instructions:

1. Combine sliced cucumbers, red onion, and chopped dill in a large bowl.
2. Whisk together olive oil, red wine vinegar, and Dijon mustard in a small bowl.
3. Pour the dressing over the cucumber mixture and toss to coat evenly.
4. Season with salt and pepper to taste.
5. Chill in the refrigerator for at least 30 minutes before serving.

Nutritional Values:

Calories: 87 kcal Fat: 7 g Protein: 1 g Carbohydrates: 5 g Fiber: 1 g Sodium: 56 mg

---

Roasted Sweet Potatoes

Preparation time: 10 minutes

Cooking Time: 25 minutes

Servings: 4

- 2 large, sweet potatoes, peeled and cubed
- 1 tablespoon olive oil
- 1 tablespoon honey
- 1 teaspoon ground cinnamon
- Salt and pepper to taste

Instructions:

1. Preheat the oven to 400°F (200°C).
2. Mix the cubed sweet potatoes, olive oil, honey, cinnamon, salt, and pepper in a large bowl until the sweet potatoes are well coated.
3. Spread the sweet potatoes in a single layer on a large baking sheet.
4. Bake for 20-25 minutes until the sweet potatoes are tender and slightly caramelized, stirring once or twice during cooking.
5. Serve warm.

Nutritional Values:

Calories: 132 kcal Fat: 3.5 g Saturated fat: 0.5 g Carbohydrates: 25 g Fiber: 3 g Sugar: 10 g Protein: 1.5 g Sodium: 76 mg

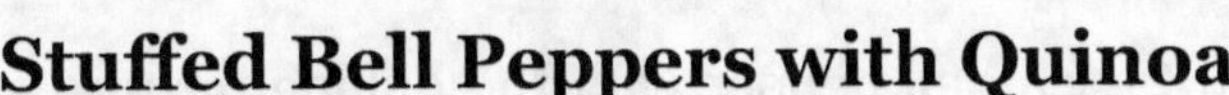

Stuffed Bell Peppers with Quinoa

Preparation time: 20 minutes

Cooking Time: 40 minutes

Servings: 4

Ingredients:

- 4 large bell peppers (any color)
- 1 cup cooked quinoa
- 1 cup mixed vegetables (such as zucchini, yellow squash, and carrots), chopped
- 1/2 cup diced onion
- 1 garlic clove, minced
- 1/2 teaspoon dried oregano
- 1/2 teaspoon dried basil
- 1/4 teaspoon salt
- 1/4 teaspoon black pepper
- 1 cup low-sodium tomato sauce
- 1/2 cup shredded low-fat mozzarella cheese

Instructions:

1. Preheat the oven to 375°F (190°C).
2. Cut off the tops of the bell peppers and remove the seeds and membranes. Rinse the peppers and set them aside.
3. Combine the cooked quinoa, mixed vegetables, onion, garlic, oregano, basil, salt, and black pepper in a large mixing bowl.
4. Stuff each bell pepper with the quinoa mixture and place them upright in a baking dish.
5. Pour the tomato sauce over the stuffed peppers and sprinkle with shredded mozzarella cheese.
6. Cover the dish with aluminum foil and bake for 30 minutes.

7. Remove the foil and bake for 10 minutes, until the cheese is melted, and the peppers are tender.

8. Serve hot.

Nutritional Values:

Calories: 203 kcal Fat: 4.5 g Sodium: 312 mg Carbohydrates: 31.5 g Fiber: 6.7 g Sugar: 9.9 g Protein: 11.1 g

 Desserts

Fresh Fruit Salad with Greek Yogurt and Honey

Preparation time: 15 minutes.

Servings: 4

Ingredients:

- 2 cups mixed fresh fruit (such as berries, kiwi, pineapple, and grapes)
- 1 cup Greek yogurt
- 1 tablespoon honey
- 1/2 teaspoon vanilla extract
- 1/4 cup chopped nuts (such as almonds, walnuts, or pecans)

Instructions:

1. Wash and chop the fresh fruit into bite-sized pieces.
2. Mix the Greek yogurt, honey, and vanilla extract in a small bowl until well combined.
3. In a separate dry pan, toast the chopped nuts over medium heat for a few minutes until fragrant and lightly browned.
4. Toss the fresh fruit with the Greek yogurt mixture in a large mixing bowl until well coated.
5. Divide the fruit salad into 4 serving bowls or plates, and sprinkle with the toasted nuts.

Nutritional Values:

Calories: 181 kcal Carbohydrates: 24 g Protein: 11 g Fat: 5 g Sodium: 48 mg Fiber: 3 g Sugar: 19 g

Frozen Yogurt Bark

Preparation time: 10 minutes

Freezing time: 2-3 hours

Servings: 6

Ingredients:

- 2 cups nonfat Greek yogurt
- 2 tablespoons honey
- 1/2 teaspoon vanilla extract
- 1/4 cup chopped mixed nuts (e.g., almonds, pistachios, walnuts)
- 1/4 cup mixed berries (e.g., strawberries, blueberries, raspberries)

Instructions:

1. Whisk together the Greek yogurt, honey, and vanilla extract in a medium mixing bowl until smooth.
2. Pour the mixture onto a baking sheet lined with parchment paper, spreading it into an even layer about 1/4 inch thick.
3. Sprinkle the chopped nuts and mixed berries over the top of the yogurt mixture, pressing them in gently.
4. Place the baking sheet in the freezer for 2-3 hours or until the yogurt has frozen solid.
5. Remove the baking sheet from the freezer and break the frozen yogurt bark into pieces.

6. Serve immediately or store in an airtight container in the freezer for up to 2 weeks.

Nutritional Values:

Calories: 100 Fat: 3.5g Carbohydrates: 10g Fiber: 1g Protein: 8g Sodium: 25mg

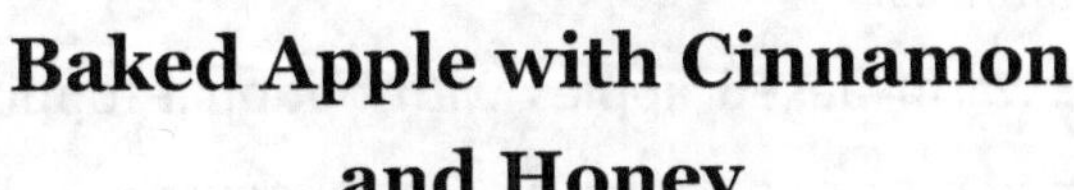

Baked Apple with Cinnamon and Honey

Preparation time: 10 minutes

Cooking Time: 25 minutes

Servings: 4

Ingredients:

- 4 medium apples
- 2 tbsp honey
- 1 tsp cinnamon
- 1/4 cup water
- Optional toppings: chopped nuts, Greek yogurt

Instructions:

1. Preheat the oven to 375°F (190°C).
2. Wash the apples and remove the core from the center of each apple, leaving the bottom intact.

3. Place the apples in a baking dish and drizzle them with honey.
4. Sprinkle cinnamon over the apples and pour water into the bottom of the dish.
5. Bake the apples for 20-25 minutes or until they are soft and tender.
6. Remove the apples from the oven and let them cool for a few minutes.
7. Serve warm baked apples with optional toppings such as chopped nuts or a dollop of Greek yogurt.

Nutritional Values:

Calories: 105 kcal Fat: 0.3 g Carbohydrates: 28.1 g Fiber: 4.5 g Protein: 0.5 g Sodium: 1 mg

---

Homemade Banana Ice Cream

Preparation time: 10 minutes

Cooking Time: 0 minutes

Freezing time: 4-6 hours

Servings: 4

Ingredients:

- 4 ripe bananas peeled and sliced
- 1/4 cup unsweetened almond milk
- 1 tsp pure vanilla extract

- 1/4 tsp ground cinnamon
- 1/4 cup mixed nuts (such as almonds, cashews, and pistachios), chopped

Instructions:

1. Place the sliced bananas on a baking sheet lined with parchment paper and freeze for at least 4 hours or until solid.
2. Once the bananas are frozen, add them to a food processor with almond milk, vanilla extract, and cinnamon. Process until the mixture is smooth and creamy, scraping down the sides of the food processor as needed.
3. Transfer the banana mixture to a freezer-safe container and fold in the chopped mixed nuts.
4. Freeze for 2-3 hours or until the ice cream is firm.
5. Let the ice cream sit at room temperature for 5-10 minutes before serving to soften slightly.

Nutritional Values:

Calories: 138 Fat: 4.4g Saturated Fat: 0.6g Sodium: 1mg Carbohydrates: 25.3g Fiber: 3.4g Sugar: 13.9g Protein: 2.3g

Mixed Berry and Yogurt Parfait

Preparation time: 10 minutes.

Servings: 2

Ingredients:

- 1 cup mixed berries (strawberries, blueberries, raspberries, blackberries)
- 1 cup plain Greek yogurt
- 2 tablespoons honey
- 1/4 cup chopped walnuts
- 1/4 teaspoon vanilla extract

Instructions:

1. Rinse the berries and pat them dry with a paper towel.
2. Mix the Greek yogurt, honey, chopped walnuts, and vanilla extract in a small bowl.
3. Layer the berries and the yogurt mixture in two small glasses or jars, alternating between the two.
4. Garnish the top with extra berries and a sprinkle of chopped walnuts.
5. Serve chilled.

Nutritional Values:

Calories: 244 kcal Fat: 9.9 g Saturated Fat: 1.1 g Carbohydrates: 28.6 g Fiber: 3.9 g Protein: 15.2 g Sodium: 53 mg

Chia Seed Pudding with Mixed Fruit

Preparation time: 5 minutes

Chilling time: 2-3 hours

Servings: 4

Ingredients:

- 1 cup unsweetened almond milk
- 1/4 cup chia seeds
- 1-2 tablespoons honey
- 1 teaspoon vanilla extract
- 1 cup mixed fruit (such as berries, sliced banana, or diced mango)

Instructions:

1. Whisk together the almond milk, chia seeds, honey, and vanilla extract in a mixing bowl.
2. Let the mixture sit for a few minutes, then whisk again to prevent clumping.
3. Cover the bowl and refrigerate for at least 2-3 hours or overnight until the mixture thickens and the chia seeds soften.
4. Before serving, stir the pudding to ensure an even consistency.
5. Divide the pudding into 4 bowls or jars and top with mixed fruit.
6. Serve immediately or store in the refrigerator for up to 3 days.

Nutritional Values:

Calories: 105 Fat: 5g Carbohydrates: 15g Fiber: 6g Protein: 3g Sodium: 59mg

Mixed Berry Crumble with Oatmeal Topping

Preparation time: 15 minutes

Cooking Time: 40-45 minutes

Servings: 6

Ingredients:

- 4 cups mixed berries (fresh or frozen)
- 2 tablespoons honey
- 1 tablespoon cornstarch
- 1/2 teaspoon cinnamon
- 1/4 teaspoon nutmeg
- 1/4 teaspoon salt
- 1 cup rolled oats
- 1/4 cup whole wheat flour
- 1/4 cup chopped walnuts
- 1/4 cup honey
- 1/4 cup unsweetened applesauce
- 2 tablespoons olive oil
- 1/2 teaspoon vanilla extract

Instructions:

1. Preheat oven to 350°F (175°C).
2. Toss the mixed berries, honey, cornstarch, cinnamon, nutmeg, and salt in a mixing bowl.
3. Pour the berry mixture into an 8x8-inch baking dish.

4. Combine the oats, whole wheat flour, chopped walnuts, honey, applesauce, olive oil, and vanilla extract in a separate mixing bowl.
5. Stir the oat mixture until it is evenly combined.
6. Sprinkle the oat mixture over the top of the berry mixture.
7. Bake the mixed berry crumble in the oven for 40-45 minutes, until the top is golden brown, and the filling is bubbling.
8. Allow the crumble to cool for 10-15 minutes before serving.

Nutritional Values:

Calories: 250 kcal Protein: 4g Fat: 10g Carbohydrates: 40g Fiber: 5g Sodium: 110mg

---

Lemon and Blueberry Oatmeal Bars

Preparation time: 15 minutes

Cooking Time: 30 minutes

Servings: 12 bars

Ingredients:

- 1 1/2 cups rolled oats
- 1/2 cup almond flour
- 1/4 cup honey
- 1/4 cup unsweetened applesauce
- 2 tbsp coconut oil, melted

- 1 tsp vanilla extract
- 1/2 tsp baking powder
- 1/4 tsp salt
- 1 lemon zested and juiced
- 1 cup fresh blueberries

Instructions:

1. Preheat the oven to 350°F (175°C) and line an 8-inch square baking dish with parchment paper.
2. Combine the rolled oats, almond flour, baking powder, and salt in a large mixing bowl.
3. Whisk together the honey, applesauce, melted coconut oil, vanilla extract, lemon juice, and lemon zest in a separate bowl.
4. Pour the wet ingredients into the dry ingredients and stir until well combined.
5. Gently fold in the blueberries.
6. Transfer the mixture to the prepared baking dish and press firmly to make an even layer.
7. Bake for 25-30 minutes or until golden brown and set.
8. Let the oatmeal bars cool completely before slicing them into 12 bars.

Nutritional Values:

Calories: 135 kcal Fat: 6.2 g Carbohydrates: 19.5 g Fiber: 2.1 g Protein: 2.5 g Sodium: 52 mg

Homemade Granola Bars

Preparation time: 20 minutes

Cooking Time: 25 minutes

Servings: 12 bars

Ingredients:

- 1 1/2 cups rolled oats
- 1/2 cup almonds, chopped
- 1/2 cup pecans, chopped
- 1/2 cup dried cranberries
- 1/2 cup dried apricots, chopped
- 1/4 cup honey
- 1/4 cup unsweetened applesauce
- 1/4 cup coconut oil
- 1 tsp vanilla extract
- 1/2 tsp ground cinnamon
- 1/4 tsp salt

Instructions:

1. Preheat oven to 350°F and line an 8-inch square baking dish with parchment paper.
2. Combine the oats, chopped nuts, dried cranberries, and chopped apricots in a large mixing bowl.
3. Whisk together the honey, applesauce, coconut oil, vanilla extract, ground cinnamon, and salt in a separate mixing bowl.

4. Pour the wet ingredients over the dry ingredients and mix until thoroughly combined.
5. Pour the mixture into the prepared baking dish and press firmly with a spatula to create an even layer.
6. Bake in the oven for 25 minutes or until the edges are golden brown.
7. Remove from the oven and allow to cool completely in the baking dish.
8. Once cooled, remove the granola mixture from the baking dish by pulling up the edges of the parchment paper.
9. Cut into 12 bars and store in an airtight container in the refrigerator.

Nutritional Values:

Calories: 225 Fat: 13g Saturated Fat: 5g Cholesterol: 0mg Sodium: 55mg Carbohydrates: 25g Fiber: 4g Sugar: 13g Protein: 4g

Chocolate and Almond Butter

Preparation time: 15 minutes

Cooking Time: 0 minutes

Servings: 16

Ingredients:

- 1 cup rolled oats

- 1/2 cup almond butter
- 1/4 cup honey
- 1/4 cup unsweetened cocoa powder
- 1/4 cup chocolate chips
- 1/4 cup chopped almonds
- 1/4 cup ground flaxseed
- 1 teaspoon vanilla extract
- 1/4 teaspoon sea salt

Instructions:

1. Combine rolled oats, almond butter, honey, unsweetened cocoa powder, chocolate chips, chopped almonds, ground flaxseed, vanilla extract, and sea salt in a large mixing bowl. Stir well to combine.
2. Using a cookie scoop or tablespoon, roll the mixture into small balls and place them on a parchment-lined baking sheet.
3. Refrigerate for at least 1 hour to set.
4. Store the protein balls in an airtight container in the refrigerator for up to 1 week.

Nutritional Values:

Calories: 128 Fat: 7.8g Saturated Fat: 1.5g Cholesterol: 0mg Carbohydrates: 13.3g Fiber: 2.5g Sugar: 6.8g Protein: 3.6g Sodium: 39mg

Fresh Fruit and Yogurt Smoothie

Preparation time: 5 minutes

Cooking Time: 0 minutes

Servings: 2

Ingredients:

- 1 cup plain Greek yogurt
- 1 cup mixed fresh fruit (such as berries, mango, and banana)
- 1/2 cup unsweetened almond milk
- 1/2 teaspoon vanilla extract
- 1 tablespoon honey (optional)

Instructions:

1. In a blender, combine the Greek yogurt, mixed fruit, almond milk, vanilla extract, and honey (if using).
2. Blend until smooth and creamy.
3. Taste and adjust sweetness as needed by adding more honey, if desired.
4. Pour into glasses and serve immediately.

Nutritional Values:

Calories: 146 kcal Fat: 4 g Carbohydrates: 19 g Fiber: 2 g Protein: 11g Sodium: 51 mg Potassium: 301 mg

Greek Yogurt and Mixed Berry Popsicles

Preparation time: 10 minutes

Freezing time: 4-6 hours

Servings: 6

Ingredients:

- 1 cup Greek yogurt
- 1 cup mixed berries (fresh or frozen)
- 1 tbsp honey
- 1/2 cup unsweetened almond milk
- 1 tsp vanilla extract

Instructions:

1. Combine Greek yogurt, mixed berries, honey, almond milk, and vanilla extract in a blender. Blend until smooth.
2. Pour the mixture into popsicle molds.
3. Freeze for 4-6 hours or until fully frozen.
4. To remove the popsicles from the molds, run them under warm water for a few seconds until they slide out easily.

Nutritional Values:

Calories: 80 kcal Carbohydrates: 11g Protein: 5g Fat: 2g Fiber: 1g Sodium: 20mg

Blueberry and Lemon Yogurt Cake

Preparation time: 15 minutes

Cooking Time: 45 minutes

Servings: 12

Ingredients:

- 1 and 1/2 cups all-purpose flour
- 1/2 cup whole wheat flour
- 1/2 cup rolled oats
- 1 teaspoon baking powder
- 1/2 teaspoon baking soda
- 1/4 teaspoon salt
- 1 cup plain Greek yogurt
- 1/2 cup honey
- 1/3 cup vegetable oil
- 2 large eggs
- 1 teaspoon vanilla extract
- 2 tablespoons lemon zest and
- 1/2 cups fresh or frozen blueberries

Instructions:

1. Preheat the oven to 350°F. Grease a 9-inch round cake pan and set aside.

2. Whisk together the all-purpose flour, whole wheat flour, rolled oats, baking powder, baking soda, and salt in a large mixing bowl.

3. In a separate mixing bowl, whisk together the Greek yogurt, honey, vegetable oil, eggs, vanilla extract, and lemon zest until well combined.

4. Pour the wet ingredients into the dry ingredients and stir until just combined.

5. Gently fold in the blueberries.

6. Pour the batter into the prepared cake pan and smooth the top with a spatula.

7. Bake for 40-45 minutes, or until a toothpick inserted into the center of the cake comes out clean.

8. Allow the cake to cool in the pan for 10 minutes, then remove it and transfer it to a wire rack to cool completely.

9. Slice and serve.

Nutritional Values:

Calories: 214 Fat: 8g Saturated Fat: 1g Cholesterol: 31mg Sodium: 122mg Carbohydrates: 32g Fiber: 2g Sugar: 15g Protein: 6g

Chocolate and Banana Oatmeal Cookies

Preparation time: 15 minutes

Cooking Time: 15 minutes

Servings: 12 cookies

Ingredients:

- 1 ripe banana, mashed
- 1/4 cup unsweetened applesauce
- 1/4 cup honey
- 1/4 cup almond butter
- 1 tsp vanilla extract
- 1 1/2 cups rolled oats
- 1/4 cup almond flour
- 1/4 cup cocoa powder
- 1/2 tsp baking powder
- 1/4 tsp salt
- 1/4 cup dark chocolate chips

Instructions:

1. Preheat the oven to 350°F (175°C) and line a baking sheet with parchment paper.
2. Whisk together the mashed banana, applesauce, honey, almond butter, and vanilla extract in a large bowl until smooth.
3. Combine the rolled oats, almond flour, cocoa powder, baking powder, and salt in another bowl.
4. Add the dry ingredients to the wet ingredients and stir until well combined.
5. Fold in the dark chocolate chips.
6. Use a cookie scoop or spoon to drop dough onto the prepared baking sheet, spacing them about 2 inches apart.
7. Bake for 12-15 minutes or until the cookies are set.

8. Allow the cookies to cool on the baking sheet for a few minutes before transferring them to a wire rack to cool completely.

Nutritional Values:

Calories: 130 Fat: 5g Saturated Fat: 1g Cholesterol: 0mg Carbohydrates: 20g Fiber: 3g Sugar: 10g Protein: 3g Sodium: 60mg

Roasted Peaches with Greek Yogurt

Preparation time: 10 minutes

Cooking Time: 20 minutes

Servings: 4

Ingredients:

- 4 ripe peaches halved and pitted
- 2 teaspoons olive oil
- 1 teaspoon cinnamon
- 1/4 teaspoon nutmeg
- 1/4 teaspoon ginger
- 1/4 teaspoon salt
- 1 cup nonfat Greek yogurt
- 2 tablespoons honey

Instructions:

1. Preheat the oven to 375°F (190°C).

2. Combine the olive oil, cinnamon, nutmeg, ginger, and salt in a small bowl.

3. Brush the cut sides of the peaches with the oil mixture.

4. Place the peaches cut side down on a baking sheet lined with parchment paper.

5. Roast the peaches in the oven for 15-20 minutes or until tender and caramelized.

6. While the peaches are roasting, mix the Greek yogurt and honey in a small bowl.

7. Serve the roasted peaches warm, topped with a dollop of the Greek yogurt and honey mixture.

Nutritional Values:

Calories: 136 kcal Fat: 3 g Carbohydrates: 23 g Fiber: 2 g Protein: 8 g Sodium: 164 mg

---

Strawberry and Banana Smoothie Bowl

Preparation time: 10 minutes

Cooking Time: 0 minutes

Servings: 2

Ingredients:

- 1 banana, sliced
- 1 cup frozen strawberries
- 1/2 cup plain Greek yogurt

- 1/4 cup unsweetened almond milk
- 1 tablespoon honey
- 1/2 cup granola
- Additional fruit for topping (optional)

Instructions:

1. Combine the sliced banana, frozen strawberries, Greek yogurt, almond milk, and honey in a blender. Blend until smooth and creamy.
2. Divide the smoothie mixture evenly into two bowls.
3. Top each bowl with 1/4 cup of granola and other fruit if desired.
4. Serve immediately and enjoy!

Nutritional Values:

Calories: 234 kcal Fat: 5 g Carbohydrates: 42 g Fiber: 5 g Protein: 9 g Sodium: 83 mg

Chocolate Avocado Mousse

Preparation time: 10 minutes

Cooking Time: 0 minutes

Servings: 4

Ingredients:

- 2 ripe avocados peeled and pitted
- 1/4 cup unsweetened cocoa powder

- 1/4 cup pure maple syrup
- 1/4 cup unsweetened almond milk
- 1 tsp vanilla extract
- Pinch of salt

Instructions:

1. Combine the avocado flesh, cocoa powder, maple syrup, almond milk, vanilla extract, and salt in a food processor or blender.
2. Blend the ingredients together until smooth and creamy.
3. Taste and adjust the sweetness if needed by adding more maple syrup.
4. Transfer the mousse into serving bowls or glasses.
5. Chill in the refrigerator for at least 30 minutes before serving.
6. Optional: Top with fresh berries or chopped nuts before serving.

Nutritional Values:

Calories: 180 kcal Fat: 11g Carbohydrates: 22g Fiber: 7g Protein: 3g Sodium: 40mg

———— ◆ ————

Whole-Grain Apple Muffins

Preparation time: 15 minutes

Cooking Time: 25-30 minutes

Servings: 12 muffins

Ingredients:

- 1 1/2 cups whole wheat flour
- 1/2 cup all-purpose flour
- 1 teaspoon baking powder
- 1/2 teaspoon baking soda
- 1/2 teaspoon salt
- 1 teaspoon ground cinnamon
- 2 large eggs
- 1/2 cup unsweetened applesauce
- 1/2 cup honey
- 1/4 cup plain Greek yogurt
- 1 teaspoon vanilla extract
- 1 cup grated apple
- 1/2 cup chopped walnuts (optional)

Instructions:

1. Preheat oven to 350°F. Line a muffin tin with paper liners.
2. Whisk together the whole wheat flour, all-purpose flour, baking powder, baking soda, salt, and cinnamon in a large mixing bowl.
3. In another mixing bowl, beat the eggs, then stir in the applesauce, honey, Greek yogurt, and vanilla extract until well combined.
4. Add the wet ingredients to the dry ingredients and stir until just combined.
5. Fold in the grated apple and chopped walnuts (if using).
6. Fill each muffin cup with batter, filling each about 2/3 full.

7. Bake for 25-30 minutes, or until a toothpick inserted in the center of a muffin comes out clean.

8. Let the muffins cool for a few minutes in the tin, then transfer them to a wire rack to cool completely.

Nutritional Values:

Calories: 184 kcal Fat: 5 g Carbohydrates: 33 g Fiber: 3 g Protein: 5g Sodium: 192 mg

---

Chocolate and Almond Butter Banana Bites

Preparation time: 10 minutes

Cooking Time: 0 minutes

Servings: 12 bites

Ingredients:

- 2 ripe bananas, peeled and sliced into 24 pieces
- 1/4 cup almond butter
- 1/4 cup dark chocolate chips
- 1 tablespoon coconut oil
- 1/4 teaspoon sea salt
- Optional toppings: chopped nuts, shredded coconut, or cacao nibs

Instructions:

1. Line a baking sheet with parchment paper.

2. Arrange half of the banana slices on the baking sheet, leaving a small gap between each piece.
3. Combine the almond butter, coconut oil, and sea salt in a small bowl.
4. Microwave the chocolate chips in a microwave-safe bowl for 30 seconds. Stir until melted.
5. Spread a small dollop of the almond butter mixture onto each banana slice.
6. Top each piece with another piece of banana to make a sandwich.
7. Dip each banana bite into the melted chocolate, using a fork to turn it over and thoroughly coat it.
8. Return the chocolate-covered bites to the baking sheet and sprinkle them with your desired toppings.
9. Freeze the banana bites for at least 2 hours or until firm.
10. Serve the frozen bites as a healthy dessert or snack.

Nutritional Values:

Calories: 131 kcal Fat: 9 g Saturated Fat: 3 g Carbohydrates: 14 g Fiber: 3 g Sugar: 7 g Protein: 3 g Sodium: 60 mg

Grilled Pineapple with Honey and Cinnamon

Preparation time: 10 minutes

Cooking Time: 6-8 minutes

Servings: 4

Ingredients:

- 1 medium pineapple peeled and cored
- 2 tbsp honey
- 1 tsp ground cinnamon
- Cooking spray

Instructions:

1. Preheat the grill to medium-high heat.
2. Cut the pineapple into 1-inch-thick rounds.
3. In a small bowl, mix the honey and cinnamon.
4. Lightly spray the pineapple with cooking spray.
5. Place the pineapple rounds on the grill and cook for 3-4 minutes on each side until grill marks appear.
6. Brush the honey and cinnamon mixture onto the pineapple during the last minute of grilling.
7. Remove the pineapple from the grill and let it cool for a few minutes.
8. Serve warm.

Nutritional Values:

Calories: 118 Protein: 1g Fat: 0g Carbohydrates: 31g Fiber: 3g Sodium: 2mg

Greek Yogurt and Berry Cheesecake Bars

Preparation time: 20 minutes

Cooking Time: 50 minutes

Servings: 12 bars

Ingredients:

- 2 cups low-fat Greek yogurt
- 8 oz low-fat cream cheese, softened
- 1/4 cup honey
- 1 tsp vanilla extract
- 2 large eggs
- 1/2 cup whole wheat flour
- 1/2 cup rolled oats
- 1/4 cup chopped almonds
- 2 tbsp coconut oil
- 2 cups mixed berries (fresh or frozen)

Instructions:

1. Preheat the oven to 350°F. Line an 8x8-inch baking dish with parchment paper.
2. In a large bowl, beat the Greek yogurt, cream cheese, honey, and vanilla extract until smooth.
3. Add the eggs and beat until well combined.
4. Mix the whole wheat flour, rolled oats, chopped almonds, and coconut oil in a separate bowl until it forms a crumbly mixture.
5. Press half of the oat mixture into the bottom of the prepared baking dish.
6. Pour the yogurt mixture over the oat crust.

7. Scatter the mixed berries over the top of the yogurt mixture.

8. Sprinkle the remaining oat mixture over the berries.

9. Bake for 45-50 minutes or until the edges are lightly golden and the center is set.

10. Allow cooling completely before slicing into bars.

Nutritional Values:

Calories: 181 kcal Protein: 8 g Fat: 9 g Carbohydrates: 18 g Fiber: 2 g Sodium: 105 mg

---

Strawberry and Almond Butter Smoothie

Preparation time: 5 minutes.

Servings: 1

Ingredients:

- 1 cup unsweetened almond milk
- 1 cup frozen strawberries
- 1 tablespoon almond butter
- 1 teaspoon honey
- 1/4 teaspoon vanilla extract
- 1/4 teaspoon cinnamon

Instructions:

1. Add all ingredients to a blender.

2. Blend until smooth and creamy.

3. Pour into a glass and enjoy!

Nutritional Values:

Calories: 178 Fat: 9g Saturated Fat: 1g Cholesterol: 0mg Carbohydrates: 23g Fiber: 5g Sugar: 14g Protein: 5g Sodium: 156mg

Apple and Cinnamon Oatmeal Bake

Preparation time: 15 minutes

Cooking Time: 45 minutes

Servings: 6

Ingredients:

- 2 cups old-fashioned rolled oats
- 1/2 cup chopped walnuts.
- 1/4 cup maple syrup
- 1 tsp baking powder
- 2 tsp ground cinnamon
- 1/4 tsp ground nutmeg
- 1/4 tsp salt
- 2 cups unsweetened almond milk
- 1 large egg
- 1 tbsp unsalted butter, melted
- 2 tsp vanilla extract
- 2 medium apples, peeled, cored, and sliced
- Non-stick cooking spray

Instructions:

1. Preheat the oven to 375°F.
2. Mix the oats, walnuts, maple syrup, baking powder, cinnamon, nutmeg, and salt in a large bowl.
3. Whisk together the almond milk, egg, melted butter, and vanilla extract in a separate bowl.
4. Add the wet ingredients to the dry ingredients and stir well to combine.
5. Lightly grease a 9-inch baking dish with non-stick cooking spray.
6. Pour the oat mixture into the prepared baking dish and spread it out evenly.
7. Arrange the sliced apples on top of the oat mixture.
8. Bake for 40-45 minutes until the top is golden brown and the oatmeal is set.
9. Allow the oatmeal bake to cool for a few minutes before serving.

Nutritional Values:

Calories: 287 kcal Fat: 15g Carbohydrates: 32g Fiber: 5g Protein: 8g Sodium: 184mg

---

Chocolate and Avocado Protein Smoothie

Preparation time: 5 minutes.

Servings: 2

Ingredients:

- 1 ripe avocado
- 2 cups unsweetened almond milk
- 1 scoop of chocolate protein powder
- 1 tablespoon unsweetened cocoa powder
- 1 tablespoon honey
- 1/2 teaspoon vanilla extract

Instructions:

1. Cut the avocado in half and remove the pit.
2. Add the avocado, almond milk, protein powder, cocoa powder, honey, and vanilla extract to a blender.
3. Blend on high speed until smooth and creamy.
4. Taste and adjust sweetness as needed by adding more honey.
5. Pour into two glasses and serve immediately.

Nutritional Values:

Calories: 275 Fat: 17g Protein: 16g Carbohydrates: 23g Fiber: 8g Sodium: 205mg

Banana and Oatmeal Breakfast Cookies

Preparation time: 10 minutes

Cooking Time: 15-20 minutes

Servings: 12 cookies

Ingredients:

- 2 ripe bananas, mashed
- 1 1/2 cups rolled oats
- 1/4 cup unsweetened applesauce
- 1/4 cup chopped walnuts
- 1/4 cup raisins
- 1 tsp cinnamon
- 1/2 tsp vanilla extract
- 1/4 tsp salt

Instructions:

1. Preheat the oven to 350°F (175°C) and line a baking sheet with parchment paper.
2. Combine the mashed bananas, rolled oats, applesauce, walnuts, raisins, cinnamon, vanilla extract, and salt in a large mixing bowl. Mix well to combine.
3. Drop the mixture onto the prepared baking sheet using a spoon or cookie scoop, making 12 cookies.
4. Flatten each cookie slightly with the back of a spoon.
5. Bake for 15-20 minutes or until the edges are golden brown and the cookies are set.
6. Allow the cookies to cool on the baking sheet for 5 minutes before transferring them to a wire rack to cool completely.
7. Store the cookies in an airtight container at room temperature for up to 5 days.

Nutritional Values:

Calories: 85 Fat: 3.3 g Saturated Fat: 0.4 g Cholesterol: 0 mg Sodium: 50 mg Carbohydrates: 13.5 g Fiber: 2 g Sugar: 4.5 g Protein: 2.3 g

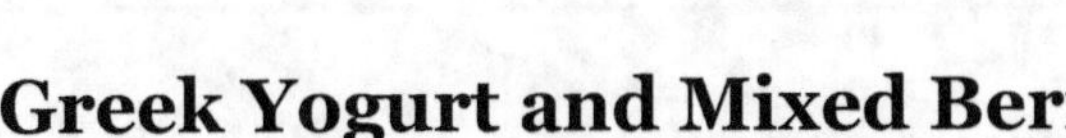

Greek Yogurt and Mixed Berry Cheesecake Cups

Preparation time: 15 minutes

Cooking Time: 0 minutes

Servings: 4

Ingredients:

- 1 cup plain Greek yogurt
- 4 ounces cream cheese, softened
- 2 tablespoons honey
- 1 teaspoon vanilla extract
- 1 cup mixed berries (blueberries, raspberries, and/or strawberries) divided
- 4 tablespoons granola
- Mint leaves (optional)

Instructions:

1. Combine Greek yogurt, cream cheese, honey, and vanilla extract in a large bowl. Mix until well combined.
2. In a blender or food processor, puree half the mixed berries until smooth.
3. Fold the berry puree into the Greek yogurt mixture.

4. Divide the mixture among 4 small cups or jars.

5. Top each cup with the remaining mixed berries, granola, and mint leaves (optional).

6. Serve immediately or chill in the refrigerator until ready to serve.

Nutritional Values:

Calories: 202 kcal Fat: 10 g Carbohydrates: 19 g Fiber: 2 g Protein: 10 g Sodium: 161 mg

---

Cinnamon and Banana Oatmeal Bars

Preparation time: 10 minutes

Cooking Time: 25-30 minutes

Servings: 12 bars

Ingredients:

- 2 ripe bananas
- 2 cups rolled oats
- 1/4 cup honey
- 1/4 cup almond milk
- 1/4 cup chopped walnuts
- 1/4 cup raisins
- 1 tsp ground cinnamon
- 1/2 tsp baking powder
- 1/2 tsp vanilla extract
- Pinch of salt

Instructions:

1. Preheat oven to 350°F (175°C) and line a 9-inch square baking dish with parchment paper.
2. In a large mixing bowl, mash the bananas with a fork until smooth.
3. Add oats, honey, almond milk, chopped walnuts, raisins, cinnamon, baking powder, vanilla extract, and salt. Mix well.
4. Pour the mixture into the baking dish and smooth the surface with a spatula.
5. Bake for 25-30 minutes or until the edges turn golden brown and the center is set.
6. Remove from the oven and let cool for 5 minutes before slicing into 12 bars.
7. Serve warm or at room temperature.

Nutritional Values:

Calories: 126 kcal Total fat: 3.6 g Saturated fat: 0.4 g Trans-fat: 0 g
Cholesterol: 0 mg Sodium: 10 mg Total Carbohydrates: 22.3 g
Dietary fiber: 2.7 g Sugars: 9.3 g Protein: 3.1 g

Chocolate and Banana Protein Smoothie

Preparation time: 5 minutes

Servings: 1

Ingredients:

- 1 ripe banana

- 1 cup unsweetened almond milk
- 1 scoop of chocolate protein powder
- 1 tbsp unsweetened cocoa powder
- 1 tsp honey
- 1/4 tsp ground cinnamon
- 1/2 cup ice cubes

Instructions:

1. Add all the ingredients into a blender and blend until smooth.
2. Pour the smoothie into a glass and enjoy!

Nutritional Values:

Calories: 291 kcal Protein: 27 g Fat: 6 g Carbohydrates: 36 g Fiber: 8 g Sodium: 240 mg